BASKET GARDEN

Mary Hickey

DEDICATION   To my father, Richard Timon Daly

ACKNOWLEDGMENTS   Special thanks are extended to:

My Sewing Circle friends, who cheer but don't sew;
The Monday Night Bowling League members, who quilt but don't bowl;
Elizabeth Daly, Judy Pollard, Suzanne Nelson, Virginia Lauth, Beverly Payne, Judy Eide, Freda Smith, Joan Mericich, Kathy Wagner, Cleo Nollette, Lynn Murphy, Nancy J. Martin, Laura Reinstatler, Eugenia Barnes, Heki Hendrickson, Joan Hanson, and Julie Stewart, who cheer, quilt, and sew;
Nancy Ewell for sharing her wonderful technique for interfaced appliqué;
Chris Bacon for her lovely pineapple design;
Lynn Swick for her beautiful grape arrangement;
Janet Kime for her adorable birds;
Hoffman Fabrics for supplying the fabric for Rose Reverie on page 5;
My husband, Phil, and children, Maureen, Josh, and Molly, who encourage and assist;
Helen Davis, who works her wizardry on the computer;
Sharon Yenter, Gretchen Engle, Nancy J. Martin, and the ladies of the Basket of the Month class, all of whose patience, enthusiasm, and encouragement prompted the publishing of this book.

CREDITS   Photography . . . . Brent Kane
Graphics and Illustration . . . . . . Barb Tourtillotte
Text and Cover Design . . . . Judy Petry
Editor . . . . Liz McGehee

Basket Garden ©
©1989 by Mary Hickey
That Patchwork Place, Inc., PO Box 118, Bothell, WA 98041-0118
Printed in the United States of America
96 95 94 93 92 91 90 89   6 5 4 3 2 1

Library of Congress Cataloging-in-Publication Data

Hickey, Mary.
    Basket garden / Mary Hickey.
        p.   cm.
    ISBN 0-943574-61-7 : $18.95
    1. Quilting–Patterns. 2. Patchwork–Patterns. I. Title.
TT835.H53 1989
746.9'7041–dc20   89-38244
                                                    CIP

Contents

*Sunnyside Still-Life by Cleo Nollette,
1989, Seattle, Washington, 20"x 20".*

Foreword

How can the graceful artistry of heirloom applique quilts be achieved in our fast-food world? After spending years working with geometric shapes, my eyes began to demand designs with the flowing movement reminiscent of a more graceful era. But the time required to stitch such quilts is available to only a few women, and I was not among the chosen few. I have always been fascinated with traditional basket designs and decided to combine a series of them with appliqué flowers, leaves, hearts, and ribbons.

After working with traditional patterns, more shapes suggested themselves. By machine piecing the basket, I could complete a large portion of the block in a short time. The few pieces of appliqué added elegance in a manageable amount of time. The flowing curves provided contrast for the angles of the basket.

In 1987, Sharon Yenter, who owns In the Beginning—Quilts, a fabric and quilt shop in Seattle, asked me to teach a series of twelve classes, one a month, using these basket patterns. The response to both the class and the patterns was overwhelming.

The Heirloom Basket Sampler quilt in this book includes all twelve basket patterns. My hope is that these patterns, combined with your imagination and artistry, will allow you to rearrange, add, and substitute to create you own unique heirloom.

Blue Ribbons by Mary Hickey, 1989, Seattle, Washington, 38" x 44". White woven baskets against an evening blue background create a clean country vignette. The crisp bright pinks and reds of the flowers complete this fresh composition.

Introduction

The first section of this book includes a list of supplies and tools you will need, along with directions for precise cutting and tips for accurate piecing. Also included are detailed instructions for five different methods of appliqué. I encourage you to try each method to see which you prefer. Many quiltmakers like to use a combination of techniques, such as bias bars for handles and stems, and freezer paper for flowers and ribbons.

Twelve basket block patterns make up the main part of the book. Yardage requirements and directions for the Heirloom Basket Sampler quilt, which uses all twelve blocks, are given on page 20.

Each basket pattern has a photograph of the design and yardage requirements for one block, followed by detailed piecing instructions and the templates for that basket. Many of the basket designs have a large triangle on which the appliqué shapes are sewn. Wherever possible, this large triangle template is printed with the block templates. The few triangle templates that are too large to be printed with the patterns, including the Set Triangle template used for each block, are printed on pull-out pattern pages in the center of the book. Open the staples to remove the pattern sheet; reclose the staples to keep the book intact.

Instructions for the Swinging on the Garden Gate quilt with the picket fence border follow the basket patterns. Directions for four other projects that use the basket designs include two full-size quilts and two wall hangings. Refer to pages 13–18 for appliqué techniques, including a special technique for appliquéing handles and stems with bias bars. Cutting and piecing tips can be found on pages 11–12, and a Glossary of Techniques on pages 90–91 gives complete directions for finishing your quilt. Throughout the book, you will find color photos of various-sized basket blocks based on the patterns in this book. These are provided for your inspiration in selecting color and in encouraging you to personalize your blocks with your own creative additions.

Rose Reverie by Mary Hickey, 1989, Seattle, Washington, 28" x 44". The interwoven ribbon and flower fabric insisted on being part of a basket quilt. The rich roses, mauves, and teals of the tulips, leaves, and ribbons float on a background of scattered flowers, creating a muted complementary color scheme.

Fabrics, Supplies, and Tools

Miss Marple's Garden by Judy Pollard, 1989, Seattle, Washington, 30" x 84". The wonderful assortment of colors in this strip set of baskets shouts exuberance.

FABRICS

The ideal fabrics for quilts are lightweight, closely woven 100% cottons. Cotton provides quiltmakers with the ease necessary for appliqué and the smooth nonpuckering property essential for piecing.

Choose colors that will achieve the effect you desire. If you have difficulty choosing colors, think in terms of color schemes. Monochromatic schemes use several shades of one color to create the design. They are satisfying, as long as you use many shades of one color and include a few pieces of the color in a truly dark shade.

Color schemes that use good contrasts in either complementary colors (colors opposite each other on the color circle) or analogous colors (colors next to each other on the color circle) are excellent choices for basket quilts.

If you have difficulty choosing a color scheme, find one fabric that you really like. Frequently, that one fabric will provide the inspiration for the other colors in the quilt. Try to obtain fabrics that have contrast in color, shade, size, and visual character. Too many prints of the same size and character will create a busy quilt.

Many of the basket blocks have relatively large unpieced areas as a background for the appliqué and pieced designs. Small, dense random prints or subtle, allover designs are good choices for these areas.

For a delicate look, cut the large set triangles from a fabric that contrasts only slightly with the background. Or for a more vibrant effect, cut the set triangles from a fabric that contrasts strongly with the background.

The photographs on the following pages are groups of four basket blocks in a variety of color combinations. They are meant to inspire your color selections and to encourage you to enjoy your creativity by adding special touches of your own.

The yardage requirements for a sampler quilt are on page 20. Each project pattern has its own yardage requirements listed. Since fabric is usually sold in 44"–45" widths, the materials lists given in this book are based on that measurement. For this reason, the yardage listed under the materials for an individual block will actually make more than one block. Feel free to utilize scraps of fabrics to create the flowers, leaves, fruits, hearts, birds, and ribbons.

If you are making the Heirloom Basket Sampler, there is no need to purchase the additional fabrics listed for the individual blocks. If you plan to make only one basket block, then follow the materials list given with that basket.

Preshrink and press fabrics before cutting.

Perambulating Purples by Mary Hickey, 1989, Seattle, Washington, 36" x 36". Purple peonies and tulips meander around the surface of this quilt. This unusual setting was achieved by eliminating the set triangles and stitching the blocks together with the baskets in the center.

Twinkle, Twinkle Periwinkle by Heki Hendrickson, 1989, Seattle, Washington, 45" x 45". Mixing scraps of calicoes and contemporary prints, Heki created a rich analogous color scheme. She echoed the themes of the blocks by piecing blossoms in the borders.

Buddie Baskets by Joan Hanson and Julie Stewart, 1989, Seattle, Washington, 44" x 44". Two good friends joined their talents to stitch these baskets in spirited pastels. The large floral border fabric completes this fresh composition.

Gone Bananas by Mary Hickey, 1989, Seattle, Washington, 42" x 42". Simple baskets and sunny colors wash the quilt with traditional warmth.

Basket blocks by OnaLee Johnson, 1988, Bellingham, Washington, 40" x 40". OnaLee's experience as a painter is evident in this elegant group of baskets. She effectively uses an analogous color combination of jewel-toned teals and plums, lending an "old master" air to the piece. The slight variations of the lavenders lend volume to her pleasing grape design.

Basket blocks by Dianne Melin, 1988, Edmonds, Washington, 40" x 40". Dancing scissors, forget-me-nots, pious pansies, and multicolored eggs richly embellish these highly original baskets. Working in pastels, Diane has appliquéd, embroidered, and quilted a whimsical collection of eggs, chicks, rulers, buttons, pins, and spools.

Basket blocks by Michelle Nelson, 1988, Issaquah, Washington, 40" x 40". Michelle's prominent use of red creates a rich background for her clever use of fabrics in these baskets. The plaid bow and the butterfly add a casual feeling to this warm piece.

Basket blocks by Nancy J. Martin, 1989, Woodinville, Washington, 40" x 40". Floating her blue baskets on a flowered background, Nancy emphasized the floral elements of the designs by substituting additional appliqué for the quilting lines given in the patterns.

Basket blocks by Marjorie Lorant, 1989, Bellingham, Washington, 40" x 40". Complementary peaches and blues provide the focus of this enjoyable set of dainty baskets. A textured royal blue fabric with sprigs of peach flowers sets the color scheme for this quilt. The paisleylike fabric in three of the baskets bridges the blues and peaches.

Basket blocks by Lyn Boland, 1988, Issaquah, Washington, 40" x 40". Lyn's expertise in appliqué is clearly evident in these blocks. Lavish bouquets of pansies, irises, and fuchsias in blue baskets create a showcase of flowers.

Basket blocks by Pat Hahn, 1988, Bellevue, Washington, 40" x 40". Pat selected a variety of red fabrics, creating an excellent example of a monochromatic color scheme. Red remains the dominant color, with blacks and whites in the print backgrounds. A Broderie Perse rose adds interest to this Victorian Basket.

Basket blocks by Maureen Scott, 1988, Blaine, Washington, 40" x 40". Maureen chose a jazzy red, black, and gray color combination for these basket blocks. Large prints spark the red and gray calicoes, and black accents add energy to the baskets.

ROTARY CUTTER AND MAT

A large rotary cutter will enable you to accurately cut your pieces. The cutter is placed flush against the ruler, avoiding the distortions caused by pencil lines. A sharp rotary blade will cut easily through six layers of fabric. Many cutting mats are available with a 1" guide and a bias or 45-degree angle line, which will further aid you in precision cutting.

SCISSORS

Good-quality, sharp scissors are essential for appliqué. Use an old pair of scissors for cutting templates.

RULERS

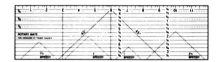

Transparent rulers are invaluable to quilters. A sturdy acrylic ruler makes rotary cutting safer and more precise. One that is 24" long is particularly useful.

MASKING TAPE

Four layered pieces of 1" masking tape placed on the sewing machine, $1/4$" from the needle, make a helpful guide (see pages 11–12). Masking tape is also useful for holding mitered corners in place before stitching them and for keeping the quilt backing smooth while you are preparing the quilt for basting. Masking tape is available in a $1/4$" width to act as a guide for "straight-line" quilting.

SEWING MACHINE

Any machine in good working order can be used to sew quilts, but one with a straight-stitch throat plate will help avoid the problem of chewing the edge of fabrics. Replace the needle with a new one.

THREAD

Appliqué pieces should always be sewn with thread that matches the color of the appliqué shape, not the background color. For example, a green leaf is stitched with a green thread.

Thread for machine piecing may be a light, neutral color, such as beige or gray.

Quilting thread is available in a range of colors for hand quilting. Since it is thicker than ordinary thread and coated, it does not tangle readily.

NEEDLES

A #10 or #11 Sharp needle is a great asset for hand appliqué.

BIAS BARS

Bias or Celtic bars, often sold in quilt shops, are valuable tools for making smoothly curved handles and stems. Hobby and craft stores sell similar metal bars in a variety of sizes; 12" x $1/2$" and 12" x $1/4$" are the most useful sizes.

To make each basket block, you will need a set of templates. Each template in this book is labeled with the template number, basket name, and the number of pieces to be cut for one block. Where you need to cut a mirror image of a shape, the template is marked "Cut 1 + 1 R (reverse)." Cut the first piece with the template face up; then turn it face down to cut the reverse piece. All templates, except those for appliqué, include ¼" seam allowance and the grain line.

Carefully trace and cut the templates. They can be stiffened with cardboard or plastic for cutting with scissors or left unstiffened for cutting with a rotary cutter.

A rotary cutter, the Cuisinart™ of sewing, enables you to cut rapidly and precisely. However, it can be hard on your templates. Slivers (or worse) are sometimes shaved off the edges as you cut. One way to prevent this is to lay an acrylic ruler over the template and carefully position it so that the edge of the ruler is directly over the edge of the template. Here are a few tips to keep in mind as you cut:

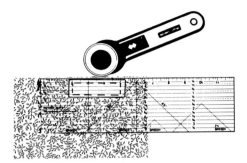

1. Use a sharp blade. Replace a dull or nicked one with a new one.

2. Always use a thick acrylic ruler to guide your rotary cutter.

3. Move the cutter away from your body as you cut.

4. Center your body and your head over the cutter. Do not try to cut from an uncomfortable angle.

5. If the pattern calls for a large number of pieces to be cut from a single template, layer the fabrics and cut four to eight pieces at once.

Accurate Piecing

When quiltmakers make a block, they sew small geometric shapes to each other to form units. These units are joined to make larger units and these, in turn, are sewn together to create the block. Each small shape must be cut precisely and sewn accurately so that the whole quilt will match correctly.

For me, the difference between machine piecing and hand piecing is like the difference between cooking on a stove and cooking on a campfire. I can cook on a campfire, but not before starvation sets in. So, I save hand sewing for those lovely appliqué shapes that cannot be made with the machine, and I have become "machine friendly" for anything that conceivably can be machine pieced.

Our goal in machine piecing is to have perfectly matched corners and crisp points. In reality, this does not always happen, but the quality of your work will improve as you practice. Do not anguish if your blocks are not perfect. (This is not brain surgery.) Just continue and do your best on the next block. Here are some tips to keep in mind as you work:

1. **Use ¼" seams.** If your presser foot is exactly ¼" wide, it can serve as a guide. If it is not ¼" wide, a masking tape seam guide is a wonderful help. You can layer four pieces of 1" wide masking tape, about 4" long, to create one thick piece of tape. Slide a template under your presser foot and position the needle so it pierces exactly through the seam line; the cut edge of the tem-

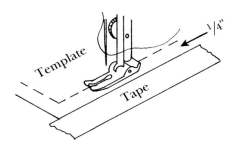

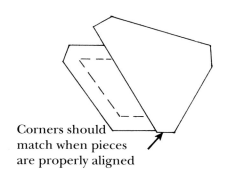

Corners should
match when pieces
are properly aligned

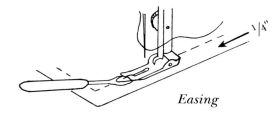

Easing

Chain stitch

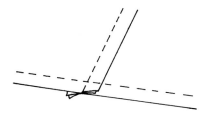

Opposing seams

plate will be ¼" from the right of the needle. Position the masking tape so that it is just to the right of the edge of the template, touching it but not on top of it. Press the four layers of tape in place and remove the template. The tape will provide you with a guide that is ¼" from your needle and thicker than two pieces of fabric. This type of guide allows you to engage both the senses of sight and touch, enabling you to sew more accurately with less stress.

2. **Match template corners.** The corners of unconventional shapes often do not match, making it difficult to know where to start your seam. To overcome this problem, you will find that the templates in this book have been drawn so that, when each shape is placed against its companion, the corners match. If the corners are significantly different, check to be sure you have the correct pieces and that they are turned in the proper direction.

3. **Ease.** If a piece is shorter than the one it is supposed to match, place both pieces under the presser foot, with the shorter piece on top. Use a large tapestry needle or your seam ripper to hold the points of matching together and sew. The feed dog will help ease in the fullness of the longer piece.

4. **Chain piece.** Whenever possible, chain stitch the pieces. Sew a seam and, without taking the piece out of the machine or cutting the threads, start sewing the next piece.

5. **Match opposing seams.** Many corners can be matched easily by pressing the seams that need to match in opposite directions. The opposing seam allowances will help hold each other in place.

6. **Aim for the X.** When pairs of triangles are sewn to each other, the stitching lines cross each other on the back, creating an X. As you sew triangle units to other units, aim your stitching through the X to obtain crisp points on your triangles.

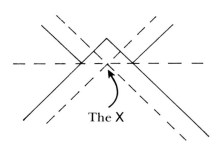

The X

Appliqué

Appliqué, the securing of fabric shapes to a background, gives the quiltmaker a wide range of design possibilities. When a quiltmaker appliqués, she first has to turn under a narrow hem on each shape. These shapes are then sewn to the background with small, invisible stitches called blind stitches. In the patterns presented in this book, the flowing curved lines of the handles, flowers, stems, and leaves provide lovely contrast with the angles that create the basket shapes. Much of the charm of an appliqué pattern depends on the smoothness of the curves of its separate pieces.

Position the appliqué shapes by following the Quilting and Appliqué Placement Diagram given with each block. A number sequence indicates the order of placement. Pin the shapes to the blocks and then machine baste them into position. By machine basting the shapes in position on the quilt block, you can anchor the pieces exactly where you want them and avoid the problem of pins poking your fingers and tangling the appliqué thread.

Five methods for turning under the edges are presented in this section. Experiment to find the techniques that best help you achieve smooth, graceful curves. When you are comfortable with one of the hemming methods, you will find that, with a little practice, the blind stitch is easy. (Refer to pages 17–18 for more information on the blind stitch.)

When you have finished blindstitching the appliqué shapes in place, remove the basting stitches, pluck open the basket seam, and tuck in the ends of the handles and stems. Whip the seam closed.

Basket block by Eugenia Barnes, 1989, Marcellus, New York, 20" x 20". An Oriental floral teams with fuchsias to create a Cherry Basket with a Far Eastern flair.

PAPER-PATCH APPLIQUÉ

In paper-patch appliqué, a stiff paper forms a base around which the fabric is shaped.

1. Trace each appliqué shape on stiff paper. (The subscription cards that come in magazines are the perfect weight. At last there is a use for those cards!)

2. Cut out a paper template for each shape in the appliqué design. Do not add seam allowances.

3. Pin each template to the wrong side of your appliqué fabric.

4. Cut out the fabric in the template shape, adding ¼" seam allowance.

5. With your fingers, fold the seam allowance over the edge of the paper and baste it to the paper.

   a. Start with deep cleavages and inside curves. Clip these areas close to the paper to allow the fabric to stretch over the template.

b. On outside curves, take small running stitches in the fabric only. This will allow you to ease the fullness over the template.

c. Use running stitches to baste a circle.

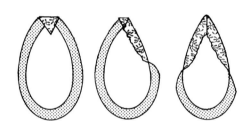

d. Points require some encouragement to lie flat and come to a sharp point. First, fold the tip over the paper; then, hold it in place while you fold the right side across the tip. Use a small, sharp scissors to cut away the extra fabric. Next, fold the left seam across the right one and trim it. Take two tiny basting stitches through the folds, including the paper, to hold everything in place.

6. When all seam allowances have been basted onto the templates, press them with an iron.

7. Machine baste the shapes in position on the quilt block.

8. Use a blind stitch to appliqué the pieces to the quilt block (see pages 17–18). Complete the appliqué; then remove the basting stitches.

9. Working from the back of the quilt block, carefully snip the background fabric behind each shape and remove the paper. Some quiltmakers prefer to remove the paper from the front of the work before the appliqué stitching is completed. Leave a small (about $1\frac{1}{2}$"), straight section unstitched. Remove the basting threads. Pull the paper out through the opening and complete the stitching.

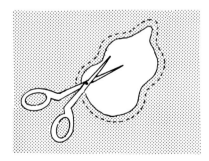

FREEZER-PAPER APPLIQUÉ

Freezer paper has a thin coating of plastic that softens and becomes sticky when heated with an iron. If the temperature of the iron is moderate, the freezer paper can be pressed to the fabric several times without losing its gluelike property. This stickiness makes it possible to eliminate hand basting.

1. Use a pencil to trace the appliqué shape on the dull side of the freezer paper. Do not add seam allowances.

2. Cut out the shape. Cut on the pencil line to create the template.

3. Use a warm iron (permanent-press setting) to press the freezer-paper template to the right side of the appliqué fabric. Put the plastic (glossy) side against the fabric.

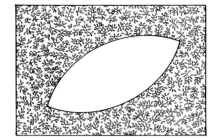

4. Cut the fabric around the freezer paper, allowing a narrow, freehand $1/8$" to $3/16$" seam allowance. By starting with the paper on the right side of the fabric, you will be able to cut a very accurate seam allowance and have all the curves going in the right direction.

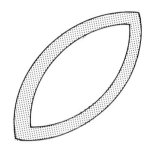

5. Peel the freezer paper away from the fabric.

6. Place the dull side of the freezer paper against the wrong side of the fabric.

7. Use the edge of the iron to fold the seam allowance over the freezer paper. The plastic coating will melt slightly, creating a bond that will hold the seam allowance in place while you appliqué.

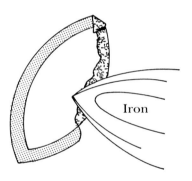

Iron

   a. Iron points, if any, first, using the technique described in Paper-Patch Appliqué (see step 5d, page 14).

   b. Clipping the inside curves will help the fabric stretch over the paper.

   c. On outside curves, use the point of your iron to tack small portions of the seam allowance to the paper, about $1/2$" apart. This will ease the fullness of the fabric uniformly over the paper. Then, use the long edge of your iron to press the rest of the seam onto the paper.

   d. For circles, ovals, and long, thin leaves, layer two pieces of freezer paper front to back and iron them together. Cut the template from the layered paper. Use small running stitches to gather the fabric over the round part of the template; press.

8. Machine baste the shapes in position on the quilt block.

9. Use a blind stitch to appliqué the shapes into place (see pages 17–18).

10. Working from the back of the quilt block, carefully snip the background fabric open behind each shape and pull out the paper.

INTERFACED APPLIQUÉ

This method, while unorthodox, is certainly helpful for some quiltmakers and produces beautiful appliqué shapes. The technique works best for simple shapes.

1. Use a water-soluble pen to trace the appliqué shape on light- to medium-weight interfacing. Trace the shape a fraction larger than the pattern.

2. Cut the interfacing, adding $1/4$" seam allowance.

3. Pin the interfacing shape to the right side of the appliqué fabric and cut the fabric to match the interfacing.

4. Machine stitch the interfacing to the appliqué fabric along the traced line, using about twenty stitches per inch. As you sew the small curves, stop every few stitches, lift the presser foot, and pivot the fabric; then proceed.

5. Trim seam allowances to $1/16$".

6. Slit the interfacing and turn the shape right side out.

7. Use an awl or a dressmaker's point turner to turn the points.

8. Press the shape carefully.

9. Baste into position on the background and blindstitch (see pages 17–18).

NEEDLE-TURN APPLIQUÉ

Unlike Paper-Patch and Freezer-Paper Appliqué, Needle-Turn Appliqué uses only the needle and the dexterity of your fingers to achieve a smooth hem in the appliqué pieces. With a little practice, it is a quick and easy technique.

1. Trace and cut each appliqué on stiff paper or plastic. If a shape is used several times, just trace it once. Cut these shapes out to make templates.

2. Use a sharp pencil to trace around each template on the right side of the fabric. On dark fabrics, use a silver or yellow pencil.

3. Cut each appliqué shape out of the fabric, adding a freehand $1/8$" to $3/8$" seam allowance as you cut.

4. Position the appliqué pieces on the quilt block and pin carefully.

5. Start by using your needle to tuck the seam allowance under at the spot where you will start stitching. Hold the seam allowance in place with the tip of your thumb on top of the block and your index finger on the back of the block.

6. Start the first stitch from the back of the block. Bring the needle up through the background fabric and through the folded edge of the appliqué piece.

7. Insert the needle right next to where you brought it up, but this time put it through only the background fabric.

8. Bring the needle up through both layers of fabric, approximately 1/8" or less from the first stitch.

9. Space your stitches a little less than $^1/_8$" apart and use the tip of the needle to tuck under a small portion of the seam allowance every few stitches.

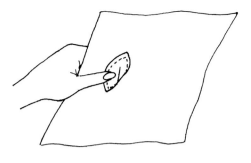

BIAS BAR HANDLES AND STEMS

One of the most satisfying techniques for creating smooth, graceful handles and stems uses metal or plastic bias bars. Bias or Celtic bars are sold in quilt shops. Hobby and craft stores sell similar bars in a variety of sizes. Most of the basket handles can be made with a 12" by $^1/_2$" bar. A 12" by $^1/_4$" bar is useful for stems and for the Victorian Basket handle.

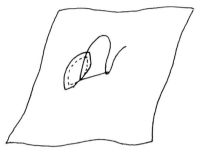

1. Cut bias strips the length and width specified in the pattern.

2. Fold the bias strip in half WRONG sides together and press.

3. Stitch $^1/_8$" from the raw edges, creating a tube.

4. Insert the bias bar into the tube and twist the bar to bring the seam to the center of one of the flat sides of the bar.

5. Press the seam flat with an iron.

6. Remove the bar.

7. The raw edge is now pressed out of sight on the underside of the tubing and there are two evenly folded edges to appliqué.

8. Pin the handle into position. Start pinning on the left side of the basket. Place pins "parallel" to the handle and "stitch" each pin in and out two or three times. This will ease the fullness of the inner curve. Once the handles are positioned, they can be appliquéd, starting with the inside curve. If you find it difficult to appliqué with several pins in the way, machine baste the handles in place.

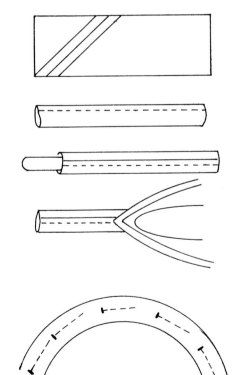

BLIND STITCH

1. Use a single thread, about 20" long, that is the same color as the shape you are sewing. For example, use green thread for a green leaf.

2. Thread the needle and tie a knot.

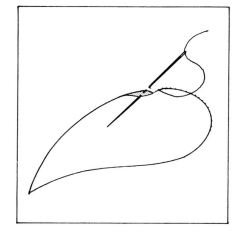

3. Hold the needle in your right hand and hold the quilt block in your left hand. (Reverse this if you are left-handed.)

4. Bring the needle around to the back (wrong side) of the block.

5. Insert the needle through the background fabric and through the very edge of the appliqué fabric. (Your needle will nick the edge of the paper template as it goes through the fabric; that is fine.) Pull the thread all the way through.

6. Insert the needle right next to where it came up but through only the background fabric.

7. Tilt the needle and come up about $1/8"$ from previous stitch through both layers. It is usually easier for right-handed people to work counterclockwise and for left-handed people to work clockwise.

8. Continue sewing around the edges, making your stitches as invisible as possible.

9. At the end of your thread, take a few tiny backstitches on the back of your work.

Basket blocks by Judy Eide, 1989, Woodinville, Washington, 24" x 66". The large floral fabric of the borders suggested the color scheme of this quilt. Skillful placement of the printed fabrics add visual texture to the ribbons, flowers, and baskets.

Basket blocks by Catherine Palmer, 1989, Vancouver, British Columbia, Canada, 80" x 96".
Catherine's adept use of a nontraditional fabric in her blocks and inner border enhances the serene feeling
of her basket sampler. Coral, peach, and forest green baskets float on a cream background, while peacock
feathers and ocean waves add textural interest.

Heirloom Basket Sampler

72" x 90"

This quilt combines twelve baskets with ribbons, flowers, and hearts to create a treasured heirloom. Feel free to add special touches that relate to your family, such as favorite birds or flowers. When the appliqué pieces are basted in place, blocks make ideal portable projects.

If you are making the full sampler, there is no need to purchase the additional fabrics listed for the individual blocks. If you plan to make one basket block, then follow the materials list given with that pattern.

Refer to pages 13–18 for appliqué techniques, including a special technique for appliquéing handles and stems with bias bars. Cutting and piecing tips can be found on pages 11–12, and a Glossary of Techniques on pages 90–91 gives complete directions for finishing your quilt.

Materials: (44"–45" wide fabric)

3 yds. fabric for background
1¹/₈ yds. fabric for set triangles
1¹/₂ yds. fabric for main basket
¹/₂ yd. fabric for alternate basket
¹/₄ yd. each of 7 fabrics for flowers, stems, leaves, and ribbons
2¹/₂ yds. fabric for border
5¹/₄ yds. fabric for backing
Batting, binding, and thread to finish

Templates

Templates for all 12 basket blocks
Set Triangle template on pull-out pattern page

Market Basket — Victorian Basket — Tulip Basket
Peony Basket — Stamp Basket — Cherry Basket
County Fair Basket — Farm Basket — Garden Basket
Harvest Basket — Daffodil Basket — Ribbon Basket

DIRECTIONS

1. Cut fabrics for block as directed on templates.

2. Piece blocks according to instructions for individual blocks.

3. Cut appliqué shapes for each block.

4. Use Set Triangle template to cut 24 triangles from the background fabric and 24 triangles from the set triangle fabric.

5. Arrange the blocks according to the diagram above, or as you desire.

6. Stitch the set triangles to the blocks, alternating the colors as illustrated.

7. Appliqué shapes to each block.

8. Sew the blocks into horizontal rows.

9. Sew the rows together to form the quilt top.

10. Cut 2 pieces of border fabric 11" x 93". Cut 2 border pieces 11" x 73".

11. Stitch borders to quilt, mitering corners.

12. Add batting and backing; then quilt.

13. Bind with bias binding.

Heirloom Basket Sampler by Mary Hickey, 1987, Seattle, Washington, 72" x 90". Subtle pastels work together with the baskets and flowers to create this unabashedly feminine quilt. The border is quilted with a ribbon and swag pattern.

Basket blocks by Noni Bowhay, 1988, Bellingham, Washington, 80" x 96". Noni's black, mauve, and rose baskets are framed with muslin set triangles in the center area of the quilt and with green on the outer sections. Careful placement of the fabrics adds color and texture to the flowers and baskets.

*My Quilt Garden by Susan McCarthy, 1988, Bellingham, Washington, 80" x 96". Susan's thoughtful fabric place-
ment and exquisite workmanship make this an outstanding quilt. Strong multiple borders frame the light, airy blocks.*

Cherry Basket

The numerous variations of this traditional pattern hint at its cherished position with quiltmakers. The version presented here is simple to construct, yet strikingly beautiful.

Materials: (44"–45" wide fabric)

$3/8$ yd. fabric for background
$1/4$ yd. fabric for basket
$1/4$ yd. accent fabric for basket
$1/3$ yd. fabric for set triangles

Templates

#1–#4, page 26
Background template #5, page 27
Set triangle template on pull-out
    pattern page

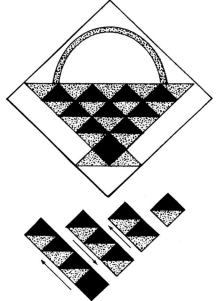

Press seams according to arrows

DIRECTIONS

1. Arrange the pieces on your work surface to form the block.

2. Sew together 9 pairs of triangles (Template #1) to create 9 squares.

3. Arrange the pieces in the shape of the block.

4. Sew the squares, including the accent square (Template #2), into rows.

5. Add a dark triangle (Template #1) to the top of each row.

6. Sew the rows together to form the basket shape.

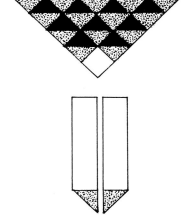

7. Stitch the last 2 dark basket triangles (Template #1) to the background rectangles (Template #3).

8. Sew the rectangle units to the basket section.

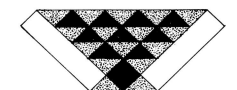

9. Stitch the small background triangle (Template #4) to the bottom of the basket and the large background triangle (Template #5) to the top.

10. Cut a bias strip of basket fabric 1$\frac{1}{2}$" x 18" for handle. Appliqué handle.

11. Sew the set triangles to the basket block.

12. Appliqué the birds.

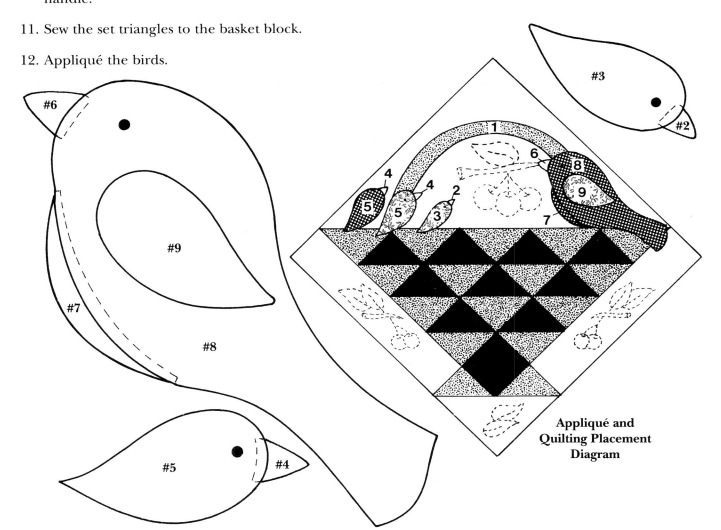

Appliqué and Quilting Placement Diagram

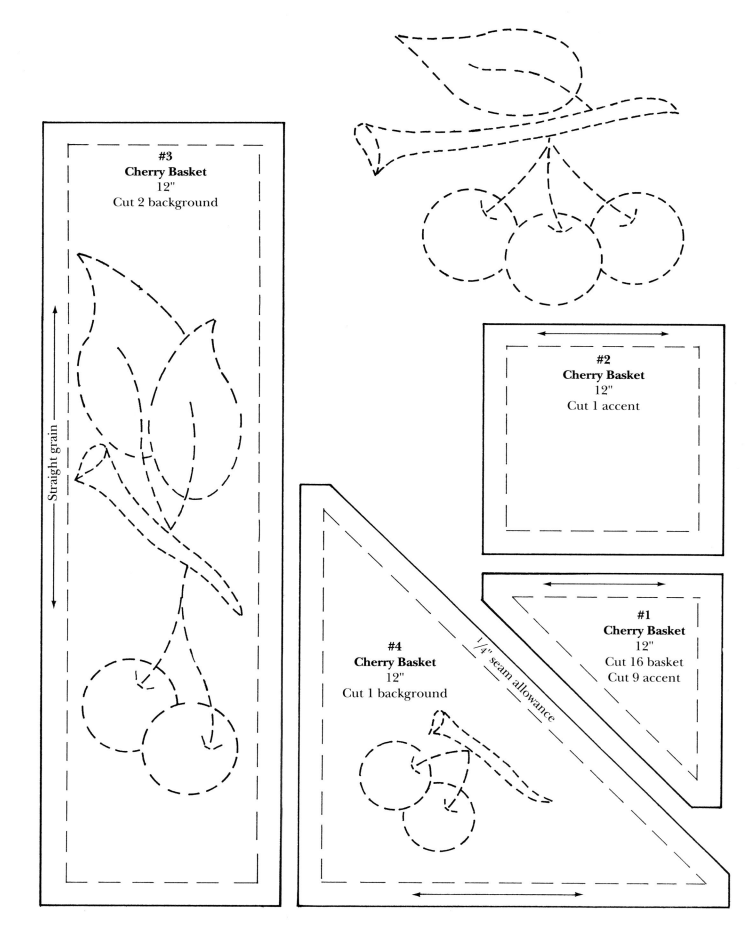

#3
Cherry Basket
12"
Cut 2 background

Straight grain

#2
Cherry Basket
12"
Cut 1 accent

#1
Cherry Basket
12"
Cut 16 basket
Cut 9 accent

#4
Cherry Basket
12"
Cut 1 background

1/4" seam allowance

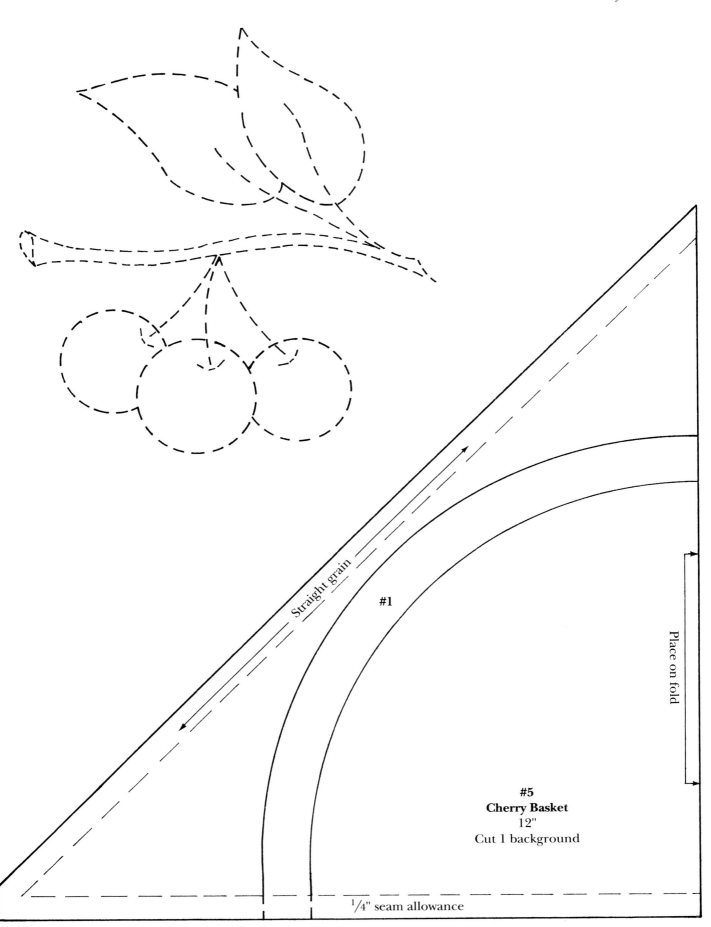

Straight grain

#1

Place on fold

#5
Cherry Basket
12"
Cut 1 background

1/4" seam allowance

Ribbon Basket

The very name Ribbon Basket evokes visions of celebrations and gifts. This traditional basket is created with simple shapes and completed with a crisp appliqué ribbon.

Materials: (44"–45" wide fabric)

1/8 yd. fabric for background
1/4 yd. fabric for basket
1/8 yd. light accent fabric for small triangles
1/8 yd. dark accent fabric for large triangles
1/8 yd. each or scraps of 2 fabrics for ribbon
1/3 yd. fabric for set triangles

Templates

#1–#4, page 30
Background template #5 on pull-out pattern page
Set Triangle template on pull-out pattern page

DIRECTIONS

1. Arrange the pieces on your work surface to form the block.

2. Sew each light accent triangle to a basket triangle (Template #2) to form 4 squares.

3. Stitch the sewn squares together in pairs, forming mirror images.

4. Sew a basket triangle (Template #2) to the top of each pair.

5. Sew the light accent square (Template #3) to the bottom of the left unit.

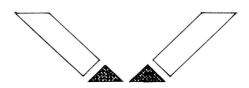

6. Stitch the dark accent triangle (Template #1) to the right unit.

7. Sew the 2 units together to create the basket.

8. Sew a basket triangle (Template #2) to each background trapezoid (Template #4).

9. Sew the trapezoid units to the basket section.

10. Sew the large background triangle (Template #5) and the small background triangle (Template #1) to the top and bottom of the block.

11. Use a 1½" by 17" bias strip to make the handle. Appliqué the handle.

12. Stitch the large set triangles to the basket block.

13. Appliqué the ribbon.

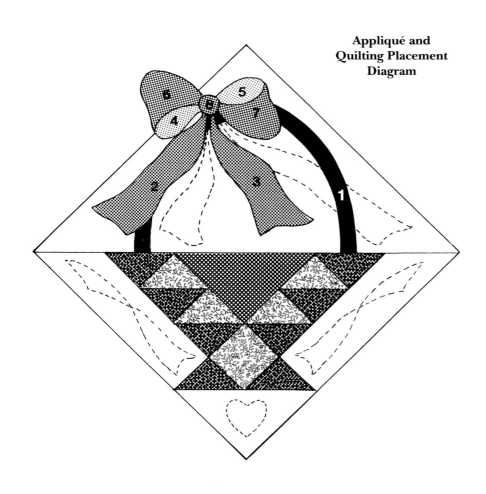

**Appliqué and
Quilting Placement
Diagram**

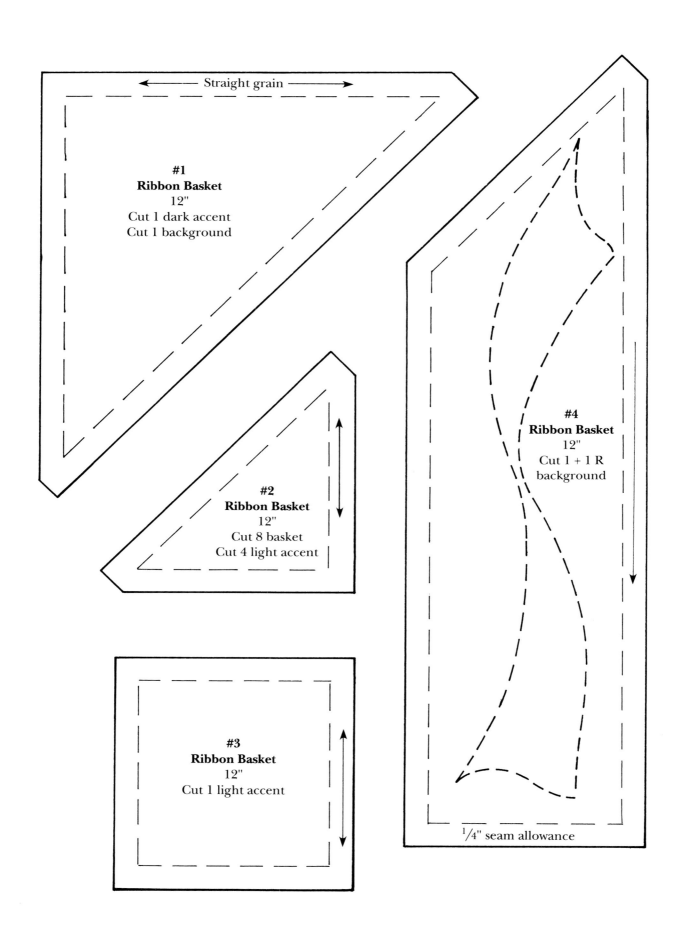

Straight grain

#1
Ribbon Basket
12"
Cut 1 dark accent
Cut 1 background

#2
Ribbon Basket
12"
Cut 8 basket
Cut 4 light accent

#3
Ribbon Basket
12"
Cut 1 light accent

#4
Ribbon Basket
12"
Cut 1 + 1 R
background

1/4" seam allowance

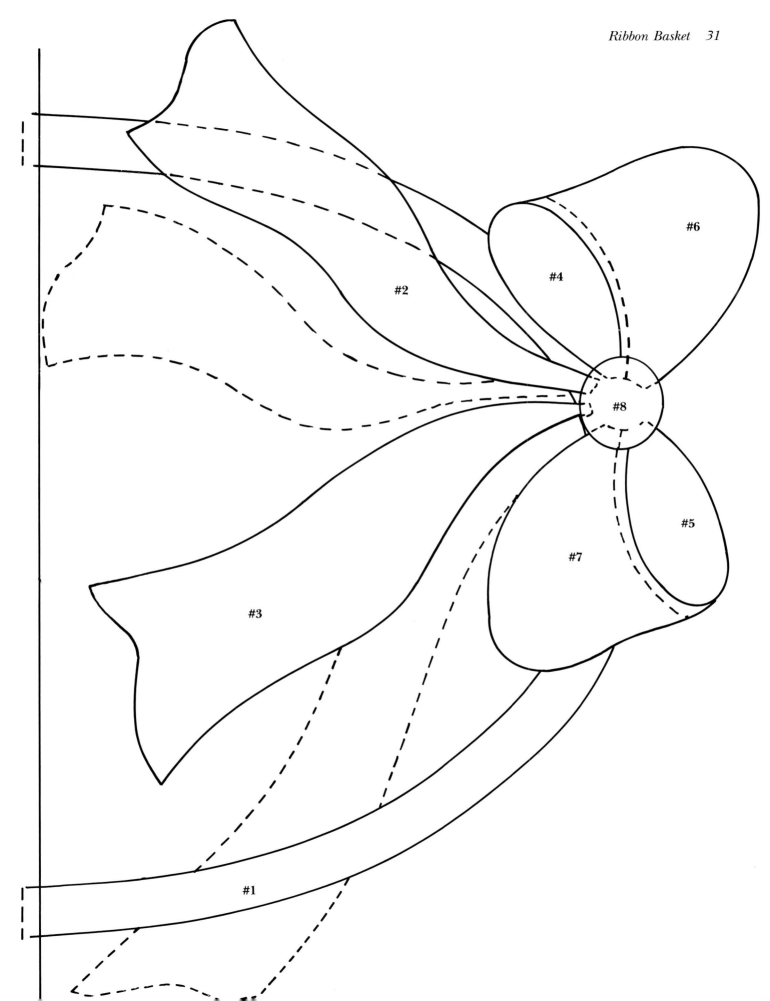

#2

#4

#6

#8

#3

#7

#5

#1

Farm Basket

The Farm Basket exemplifies the tradition of patchwork designs inspired by ordinary objects. This appealing pattern is easy to sew and can be filled with appliquéd flowers or decorated with a cheery bow, as shown in Bandana Basket on page 77.

Materials: (44"–45" wide fabric)

$^3/_8$ yd. fabric for background
$^1/_4$ yd. fabric for basket
$^1/_3$ yd. accent fabric for band and
    handle
$^1/_8$ yd. each or scraps of 4 fabrics for
    flowers, stems, and leaves
$^1/_3$ yd. fabric for set triangles

Templates

#1–#4, pages 34–35
Background template #5 on pull-out
    pattern page
Set Triangle template on pull-out
    pattern page

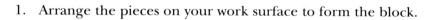

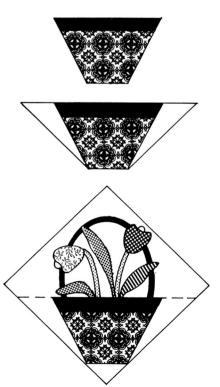

DIRECTIONS

1. Arrange the pieces on your work surface to form the block.

2. Sew the accent strip (Template #2) to the top of the basket shape (Template #1).

3. Stitch the thin background triangles (Template #3) to the basket unit. When pressed, the tops of the triangles should form a continuous straight line with the top of the basket.

4. Stitch the small background triangle (Template #4) to the base of the basket.

5. Sew the large background triangle (Template #5) to the top of the basket.

6. Sew the set triangles to the block.

7. Appliqué the handle, using a bias strip 1$^1/_2$" by 19".

8. Appliqué the stems, using 2 bias strips, each 1" x 8".

9. Appliqué the flowers and leaves.

#4

#5

#8

#2

#9

#1

#3

#10

#7

#6

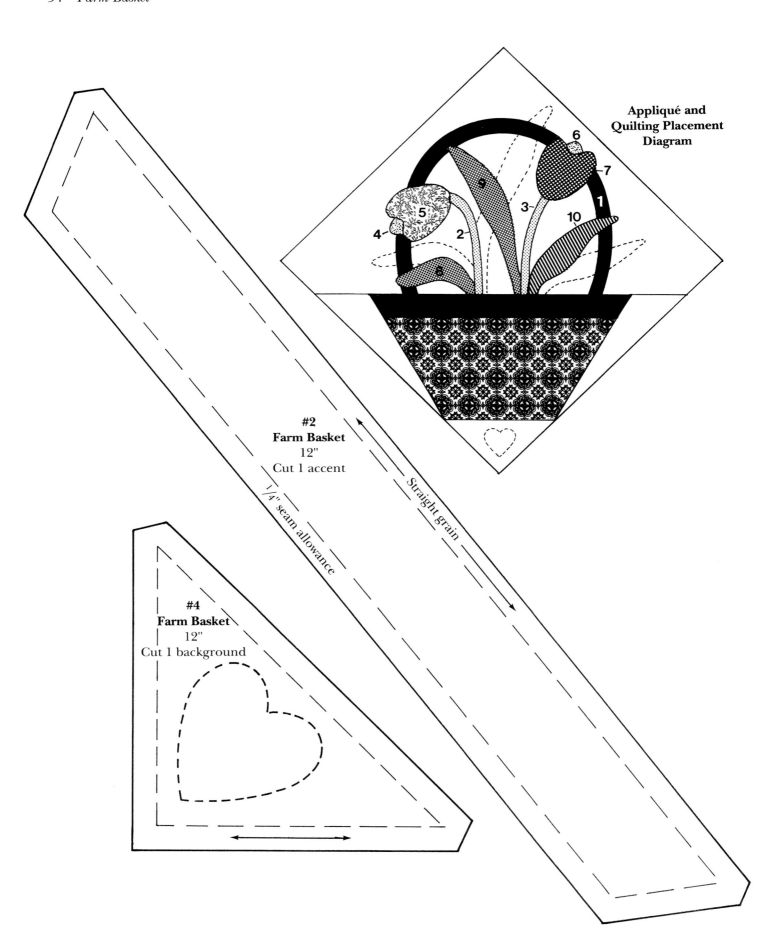

Appliqué and Quilting Placement Diagram

#2
Farm Basket
12"
Cut 1 accent

1/4" seam allowance

Straight grain

#4
Farm Basket
12"
Cut 1 background

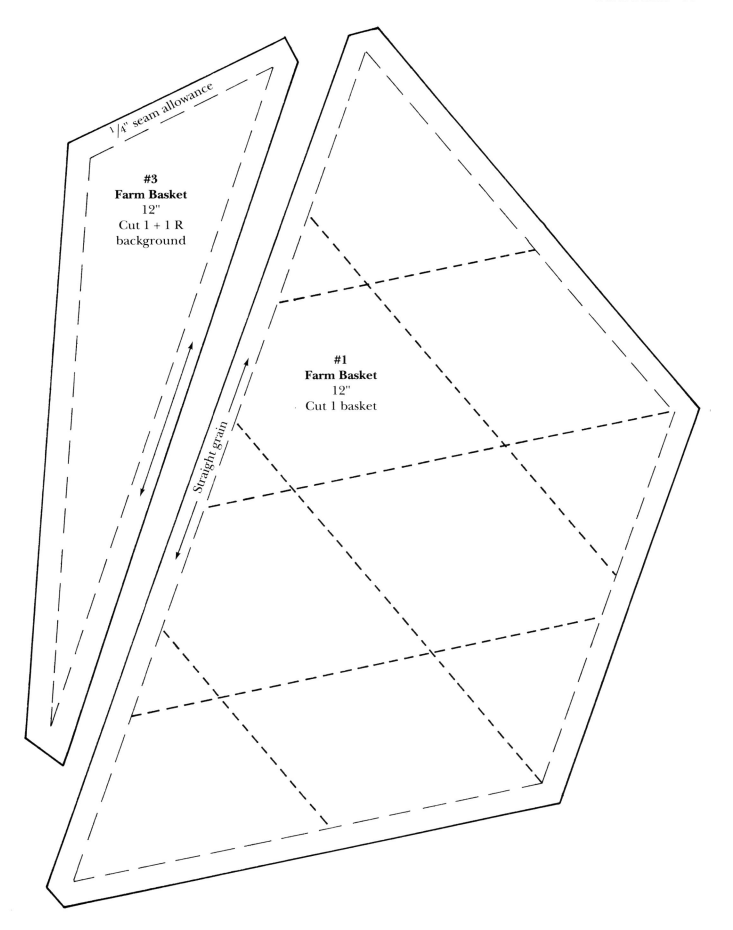

¼" seam allowance

#3
Farm Basket
12"
Cut 1 + 1 R
background

Straight grain

#1
Farm Basket
12"
Cut 1 basket

County Fair Basket

The showing and sharing of one's skills at the fair has always been a part of rural life and the quilting tradition. The County Fair Basket utilizes a band of triangles to create the woven edge. The simple appliqué heart fills the large triangle that forms the base of the basket.

Materials: (44"–45" wide fabric)

$^3/_8$ yd. fabric for background
$^1/_4$ yd. fabric for basket
$^1/_8$ yd. dark accent fabric for small triangles
$^1/_8$ yd. light accent fabric for small triangles
$^1/_8$ yd. or scrap of fabric for heart
$^1/_3$ yd. fabric for set triangles

Templates

#1–#4, pages 38–39.
Background template #5, page 38
Set Triangle template on pull-out pattern page

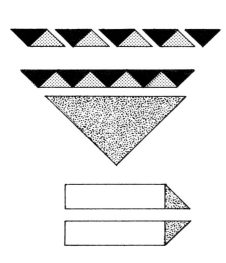

DIRECTIONS

1. Arrange the pieces on your work surface to form the block.

2. Sew a dark accent triangle to each light accent triangle (Template #1).

3. Stitch the triangle pairs to each other in a row.

4. Sew the extra dark triangle (Template #1) on the end of the row.

5. Sew the triangle row to the large basket triangle (Template #3).

6. Stitch the small basket triangles (Template #1) to the long background rectangles (Template #4).

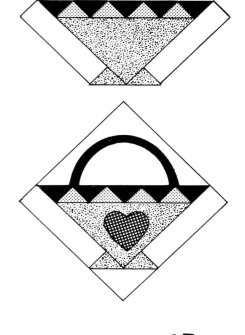

7. Stitch these units to the sides of the basket unit.

8. Sew the small background triangle (Template #2) to the bottom of the basket unit.

9. Sew on the large background triangle (Template #5).

10. Appliqué the heart to the basket.

11. Appliqué the handle to the top of the basket, using a bias strip 1$\frac{1}{2}$" by 15".

12. Attach the set triangles.

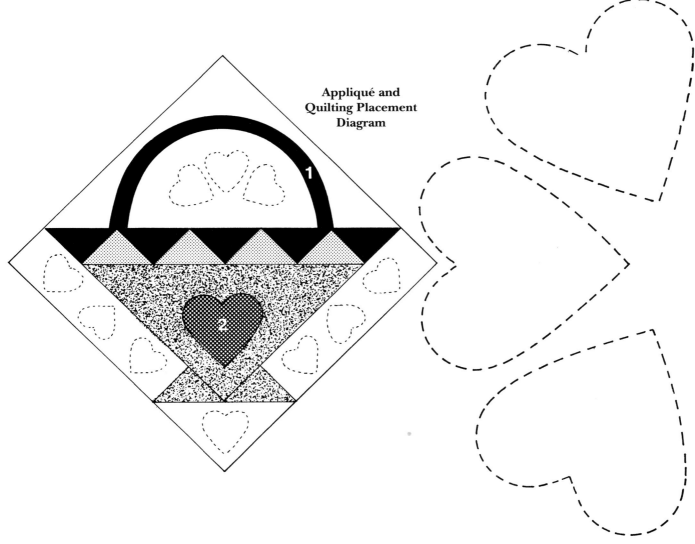

Appliqué and Quilting Placement Diagram

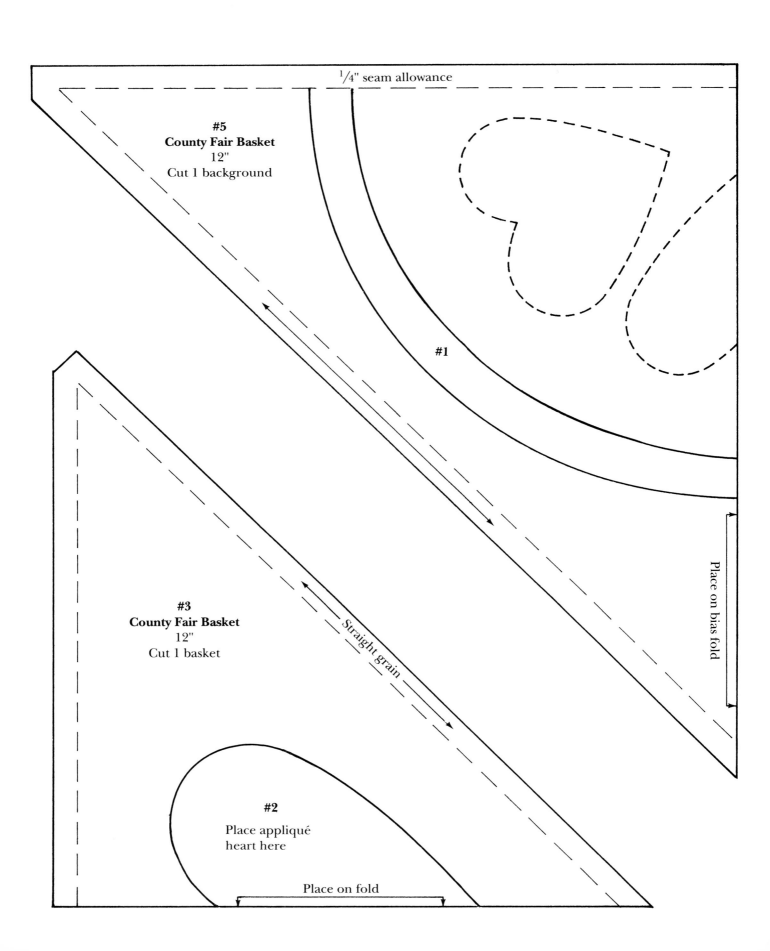

1/4" seam allowance

#5
County Fair Basket
12"
Cut 1 background

#1

Place on bias fold

#3
County Fair Basket
12"
Cut 1 basket

Straight grain

#2

Place appliqué
heart here

Place on fold

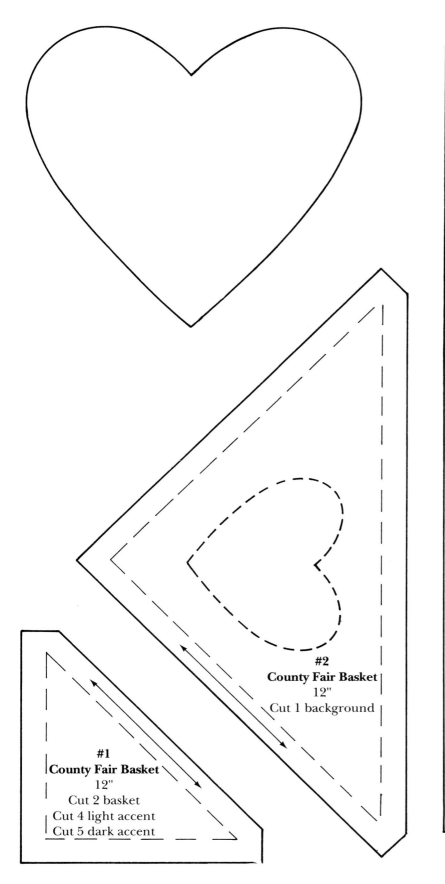

#2
County Fair Basket
12"
Cut 1 background

#1
County Fair Basket
12"
Cut 2 basket
Cut 4 light accent
Cut 5 dark accent

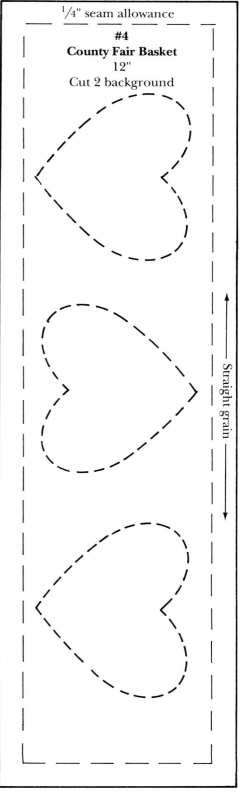

¹/4" seam allowance

#4
County Fair Basket
12"
Cut 2 background

Straight grain

Stamp Basket

The dainty Stamp Basket is simple to construct and fascinating to arrange into a quilt top. The blocks can be separated by set blocks for an old-fashioned look, or they can be set together without sashing to create delightful secondary patterns.

Materials: (44"–45" wide fabric)

¹/₄ yd. fabric for background
9" squares of 4 different fabrics for baskets
¹/₈ yd. or scraps of 4 fabrics for hearts
¹/₃ yd. fabric for set triangles

Templates

#1–#5, pages 42–43
Set Triangle template on pull-out pattern page

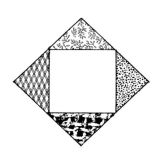

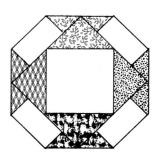

DIRECTIONS

1. Arrange the pieces on your work surface to form the block.

2. Sew the large basket triangles (Template #2) to the background square (Template #1).

3. Stitch the small basket triangles (Template #4) to the background rectangles (Template #3). Be careful to keep them in the proper order so they will match the right basket. Make 4 units like this.

4. Sew these units to the center section.

5. Sew the background triangles (Template #5) to the base of the baskets to complete the block.

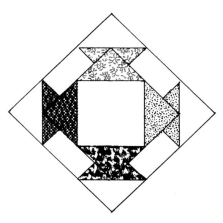

6. Add the set triangles.

7. Use 4 bias strips, each 1" x 7", to make handles. Appliqué handles.

8. Appliqué hearts.

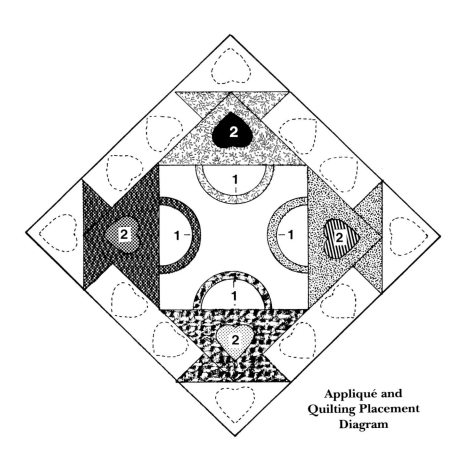

Appliqué and Quilting Placement Diagram

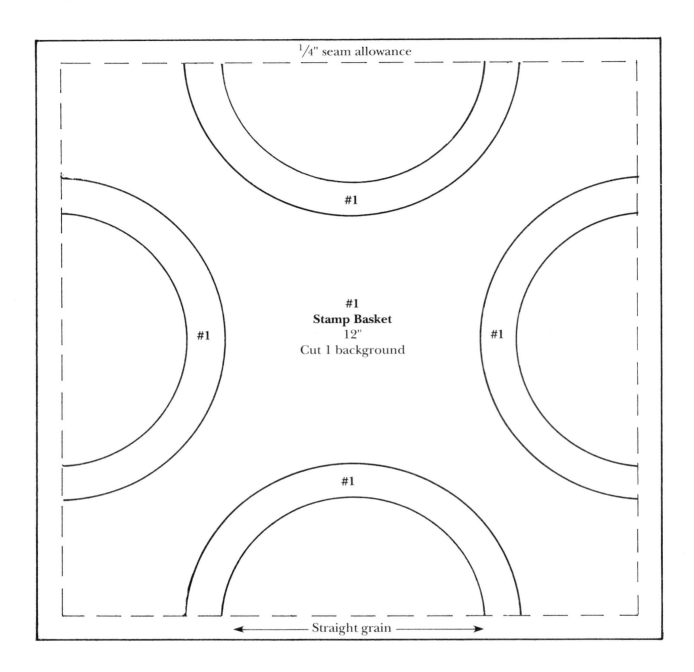

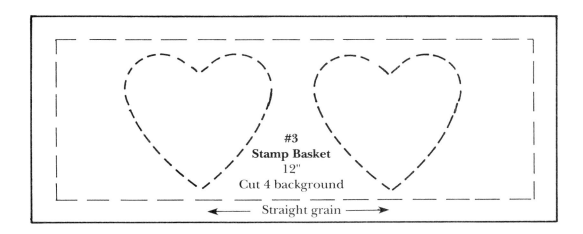

#3
Stamp Basket
12"
Cut 4 background

← Straight grain →

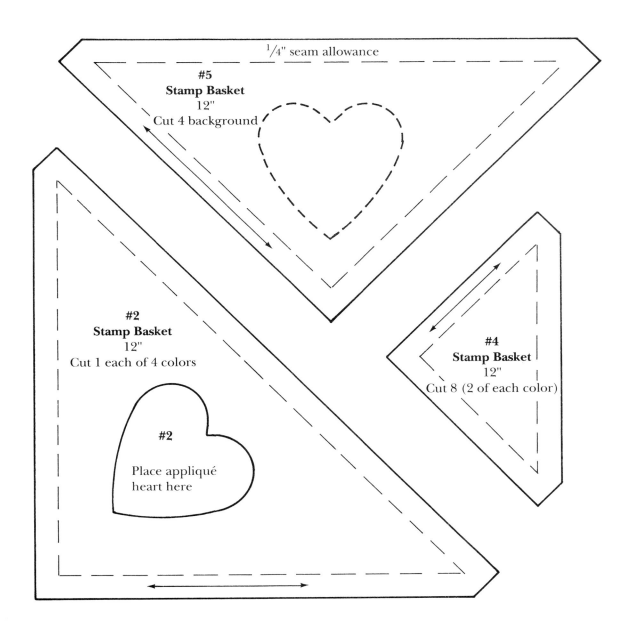

¹/₄" seam allowance

#5
Stamp Basket
12"
Cut 4 background

#2
Stamp Basket
12"
Cut 1 each of 4 colors

#2

Place appliqué
heart here

#4
Stamp Basket
12"
Cut 8 (2 of each color)

Market Basket

With its bright band of Seminole checks, the Market Basket celebrates the loveliness of everyday household items. It makes a handsome addition to a basket sampler, or combine it with its country cousin, the Farm Basket, to make an impressive full-size quilt (see page 32).

Materials: (44"–45" wide fabric)

$^3/_8$ yd. fabric for background
$^1/_4$ yd. fabric for basket
$^1/_8$ yd. dark accent fabric for
    Seminole band
$^1/_8$ yd. light accent fabric for
    Seminole band
$^1/_8$ yd. each or scraps of 2 fabrics for
    bow
$^1/_3$ yd. fabric for set triangles

Templates

#1–#4, pages 45–47
Background template on pull-out
    pattern page
Set Triangle template on pull-out
    pattern page

DIRECTIONS

1. Arrange the pieces on your work surface to form the block.

2. Cut 1 strip light accent fabric $1^1/_2$" x 18".

3. Cut 2 strips dark accent fabric, each $1^1/_2$" x 18".

4. Sew the light strip between the dark strips and press toward the dark.

5. Cut the strip unit into $1^1/_2$" segments.

6. Tilt the segments on point and stitch them together, matching the points where the light corners meet each other.

7. Position Template #2 on the strip of squares with the center line of template between 2 light squares. There should be 4 squares on either side of the center with points of dark accent fabric sticking out above and below the template. Cut around the template to create the band that goes across the top of the basket.

8. Stitch the band to the basket top (Template #1), being careful to sew next to, but not on top of, the points of the light squares. Sew with the band of squares on top.

9. Sew the long thin side triangles (Template #3) to the basket unit.

10. Stitch the small background triangle (Template #4) and large background triangle (Template #5) to the bottom and top of the basket.

11. Appliqué the handle, using a 1½" x 18" bias strip.

12. Sew the set triangles to the basket block.

13. Appliqué the bow.

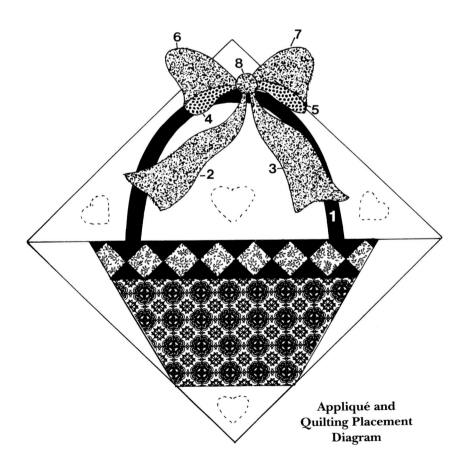

Appliqué and Quilting Placement Diagram

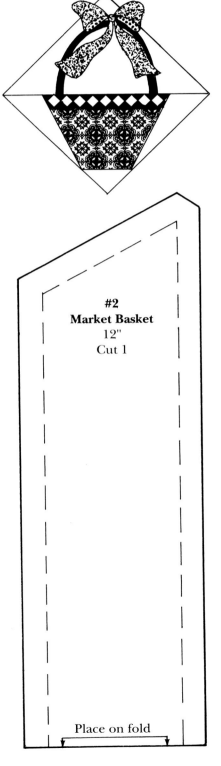

#2
Market Basket
12"
Cut 1

Place on fold

#7

#5

#3

#8

#6

#4

#2

#1

#4
Market Basket
12"
Cut 1 background

Straight grain

¼" seam allowance

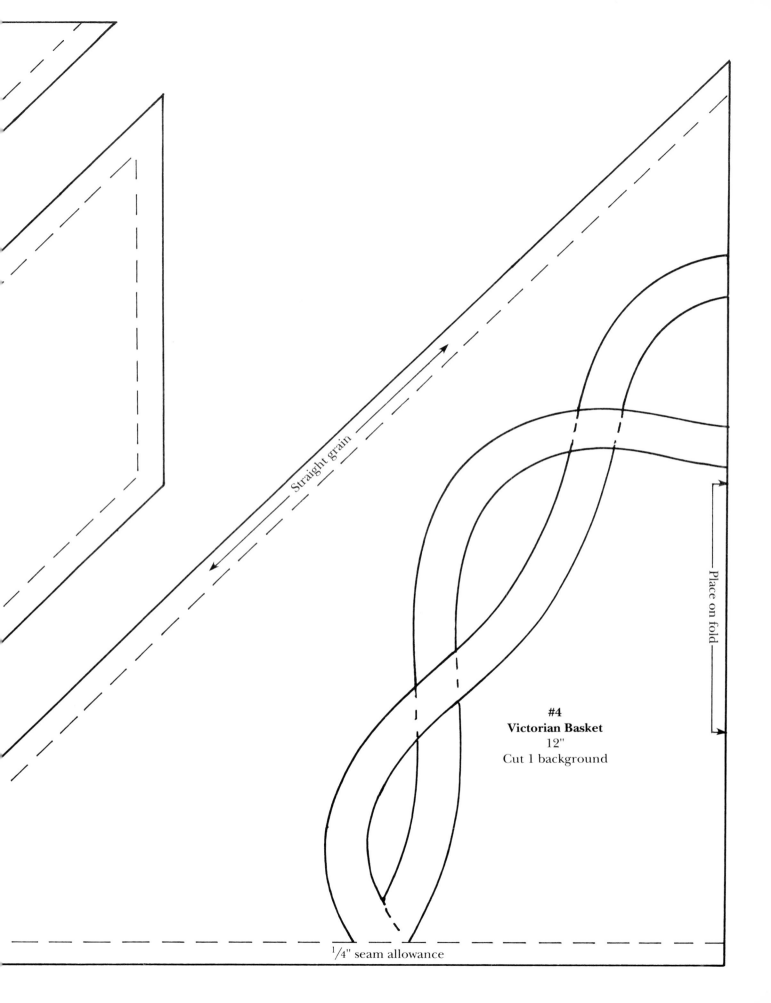

Straight grain

Place on fold

#4
Victorian Basket
12"
Cut 1 background

1/4" seam allowance

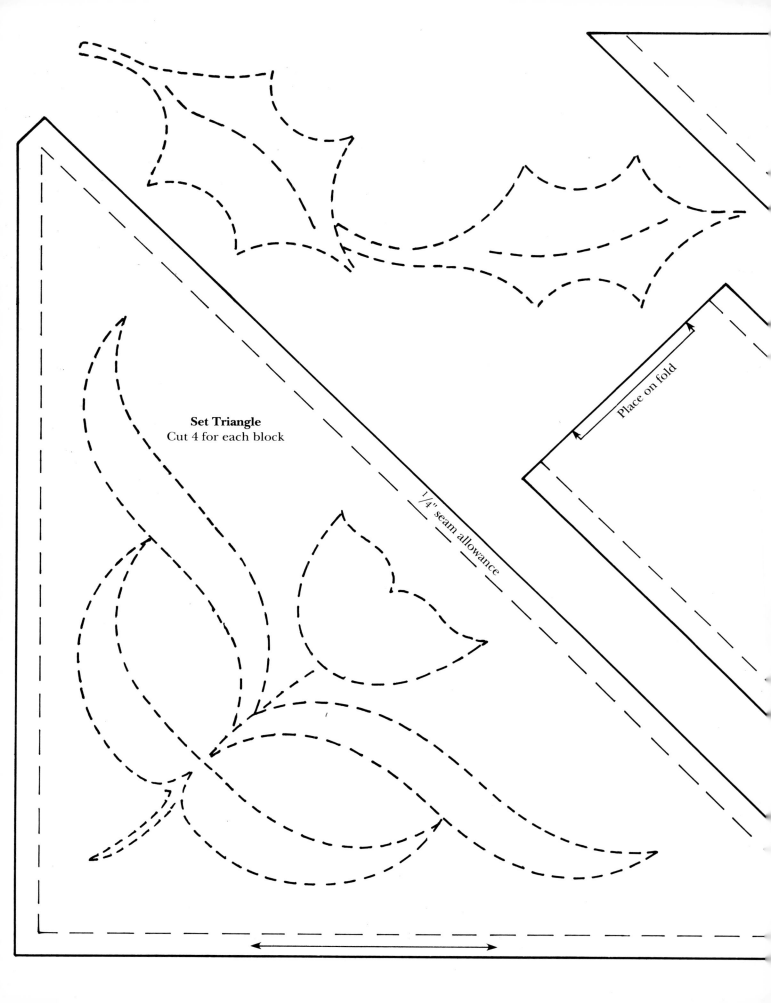

Set Triangle
Cut 4 for each block

1/4" seam allowance

Place on fold

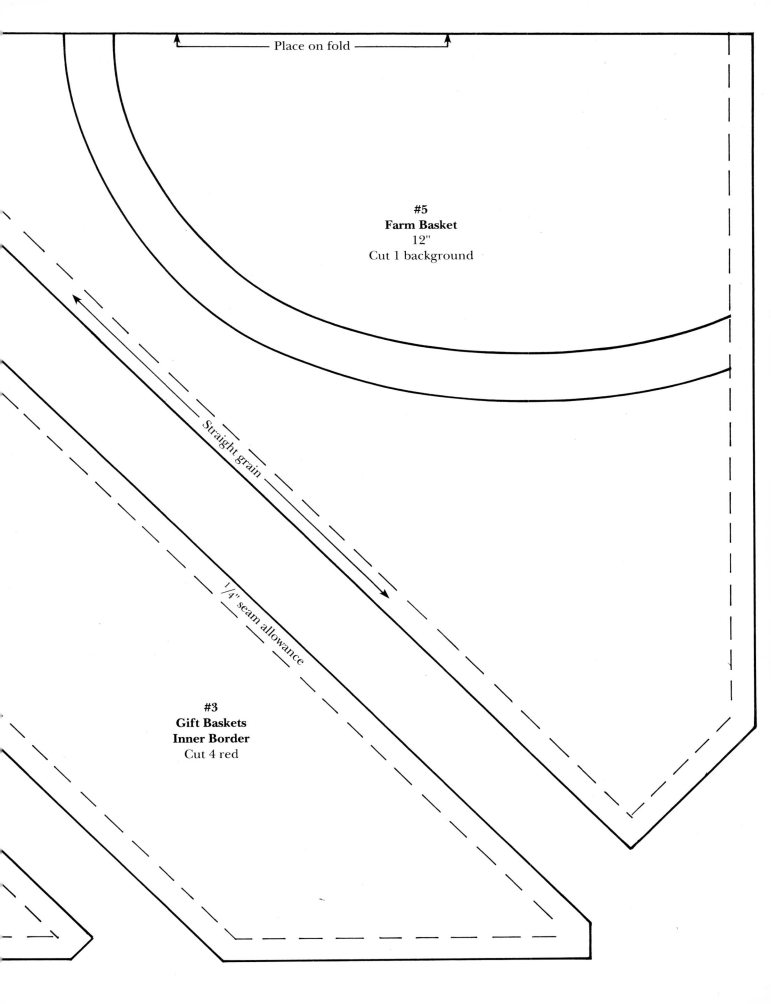

Place on fold

#5
Farm Basket
12"
Cut 1 background

Straight grain

¼" seam allowance

#3
Gift Baskets
Inner Border
Cut 4 red

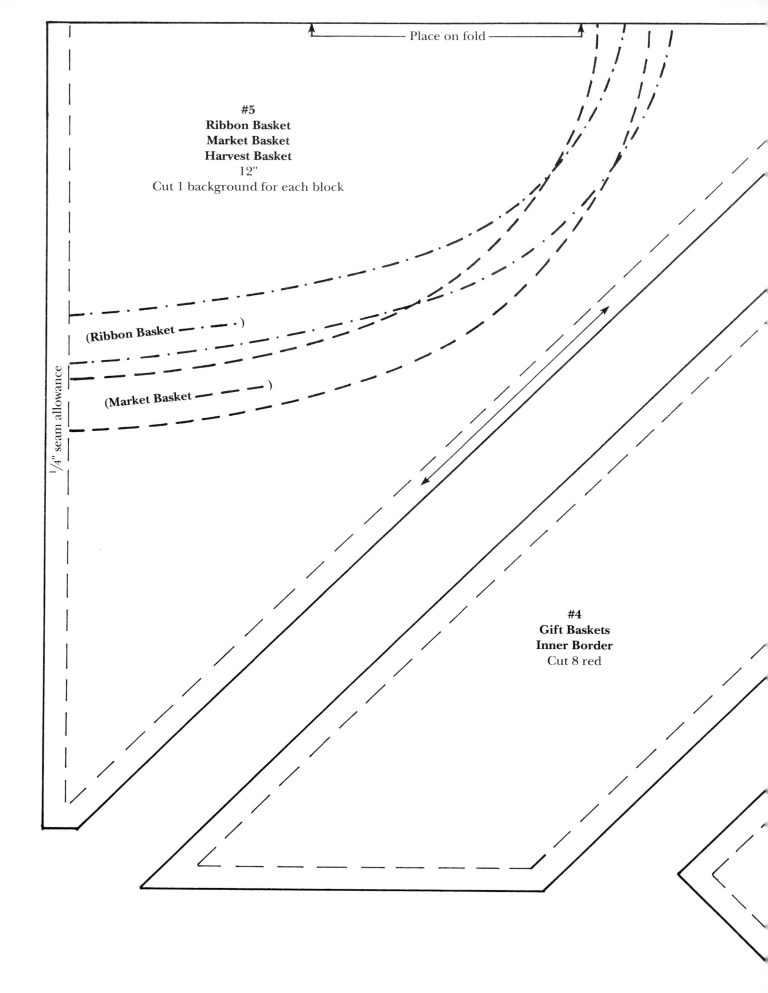

Place on fold

#5
Ribbon Basket
Market Basket
Harvest Basket
12"
Cut 1 background for each block

(Ribbon Basket — · — · —)

(Market Basket — — —)

¹/₄" seam allowance

#4
Gift Baskets
Inner Border
Cut 8 red

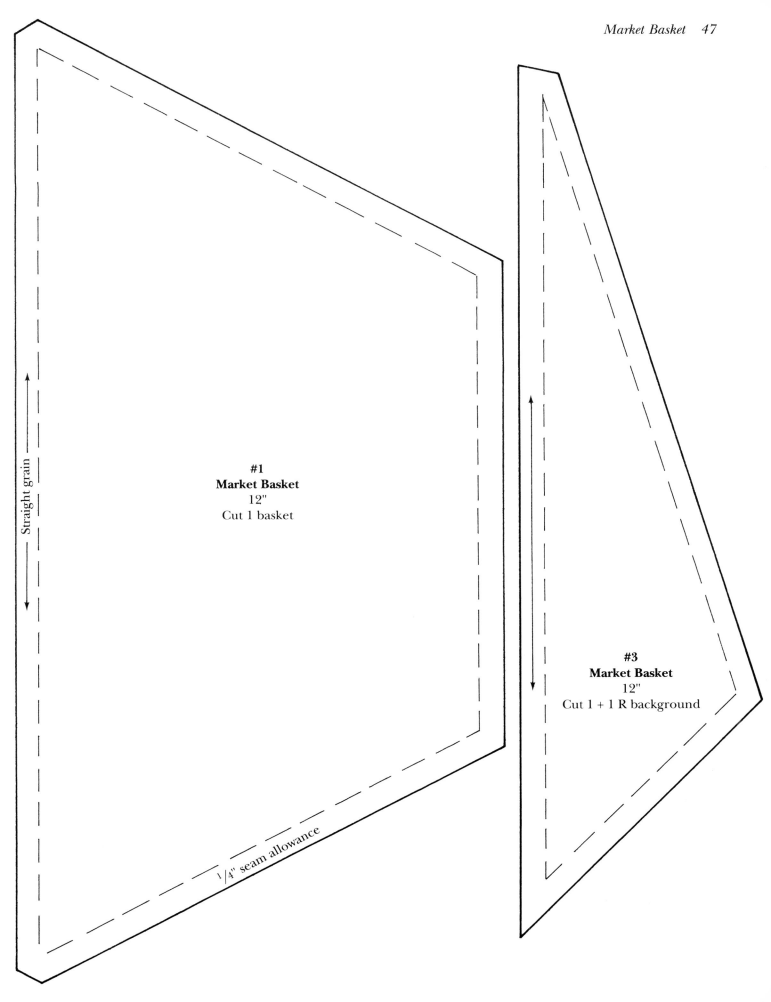

Straight grain

#1
Market Basket
12"
Cut 1 basket

¹/4" seam allowance

#3
Market Basket
12"
Cut 1 + 1 R background

Harvest Basket

In farming communities, autumn is a time to reap the results of many months of work. The abundant arrangement of fruit in Harvest Basket makes it an appropriate autumn wall hanging or a beautiful addition to a basket sampler. The construction is simple and the appliqué is surprisingly easy.

Materials: (44"–45" wide fabric)

$^3/_8$ yd. fabric for background
$^1/_4$ yd. fabric for basket
$^1/_8$ yd. accent fabric for basket
$^1/_8$ yd. each or scraps of 5 fabrics for fruit
$^1/_3$ yd. fabric for set triangles

Templates

#1–#4, pages 49–51
Background template #5 on pull-out pattern page
Set Triangle template on pull-out pattern page

DIRECTIONS

1. Arrange the pieces on your work surface to form the block.

2. Sew the squares (Template #1) into rows.

3. Add a basket triangle (Template #2) to the top of each row of squares.

4. Sew the last basket triangle (Template #1) to the right side of the small unit.

5. Stitch the rows of squares into the basket shape, matching the corners.

6. Sew the accent triangles (Template #2) to the long background pieces (Template #3).

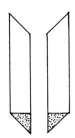

7. Stitch these units to the basket section.

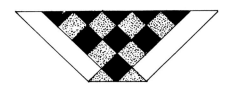

8. Sew the small triangle (Template #4) onto the base of the basket.

9. Appliqué fruit to the large triangle (Template #5).

10. Stitch the large fruit triangle to the basket section.

11. Appliqué the handles, using 2 bias strips 1¼" x 7".

12. Stitch the set triangles to the basket block.

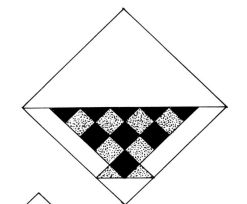

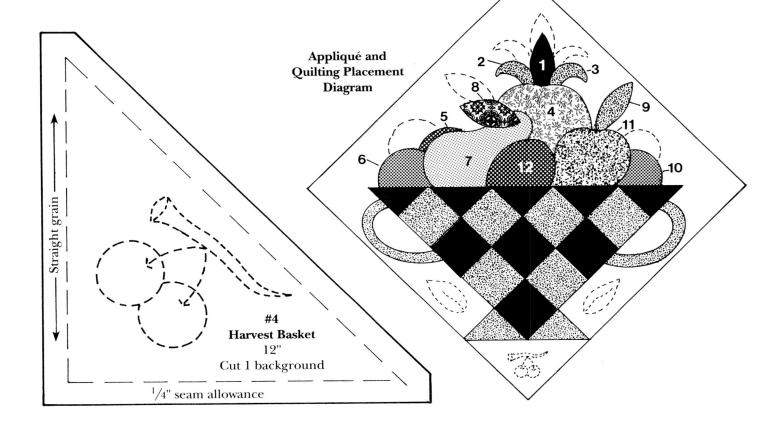

Straight grain

Appliqué and Quilting Placement Diagram

#4
Harvest Basket
12"
Cut 1 background

¼" seam allowance

#9

#3

#10

#1

#11

#2

#4

#8

#12

1/4" seam allowance

#1
Harvest Basket
12"
Cut 4 basket
Cut 6 accent

#7

#5

#6

Pineapple design by Chris Bacon

Connect with right side, page 51

Straight grain

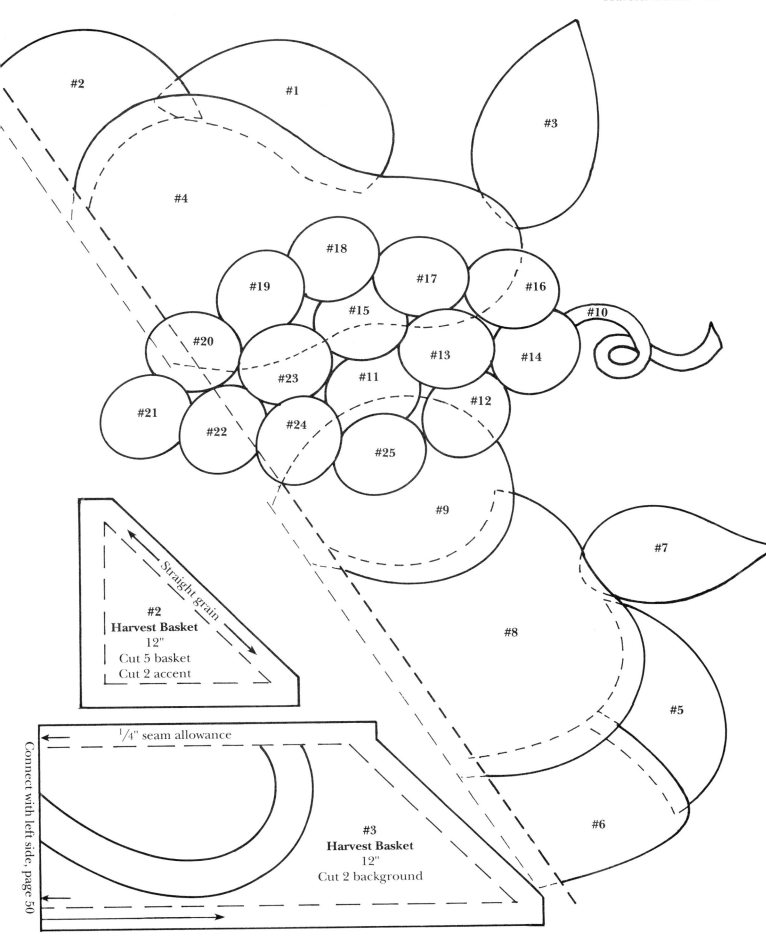

#2

#1

#3

#4

#18

#19

#17

#16

#15

#10

#20

#13

#14

#23

#11

#21

#22

#24

#12

#25

#9

#7

Straight grain

#2
Harvest Basket
12"
Cut 5 basket
Cut 2 accent

#8

#5

¹/₄" seam allowance

#6

#3
Harvest Basket
12"
Cut 2 background

Connect with left side, page 50

Garden Basket

The Garden Basket is a graceful pattern, endearing in its simplicity and versatile in many settings. Lovely with a bouquet of pansies or a ribbon, or elegant on its own, it is a delightful basket to stitch.

Materials: (44"–45" wide fabric)

$3/8$ yd. fabric for background
$1/4$ yd. fabric for basket
$1/8$ yd. accent fabric for bands on basket
$1/8$ yd. each or scraps of 5 fabrics for pansies
$1/3$ yd. fabric for set triangles

Templates

#1–#6, pages 53–55
Set Triangle template on pull-out pattern page

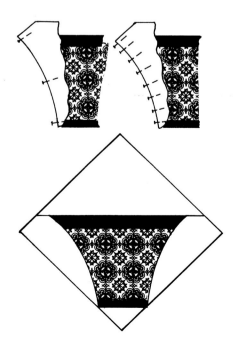

DIRECTIONS

1. Arrange the pieces on your work surface to form the block.

2. Sew the accent strips (templates #1 and #2) to the top and bottom of the basket section (Template #3).

3. Pin the background side pieces (Template #4) to the basket unit. Place a pin at the top, bottom, and center. Then, put several more pins in to ease the pieces together. Stitch with the background pieces on top.

4. Sew the large background triangle (Template #6) and small background triangle (Template #5) to the top and bottom of the basket unit.

5. Sew the set triangles to the basket block.

6. Appliqué the handle, using a $1^1/2$" x 16" bias strip.

7. Appliqué the stems, using 3 bias strips, each 1" x 9".

8. Appliqué flowers.

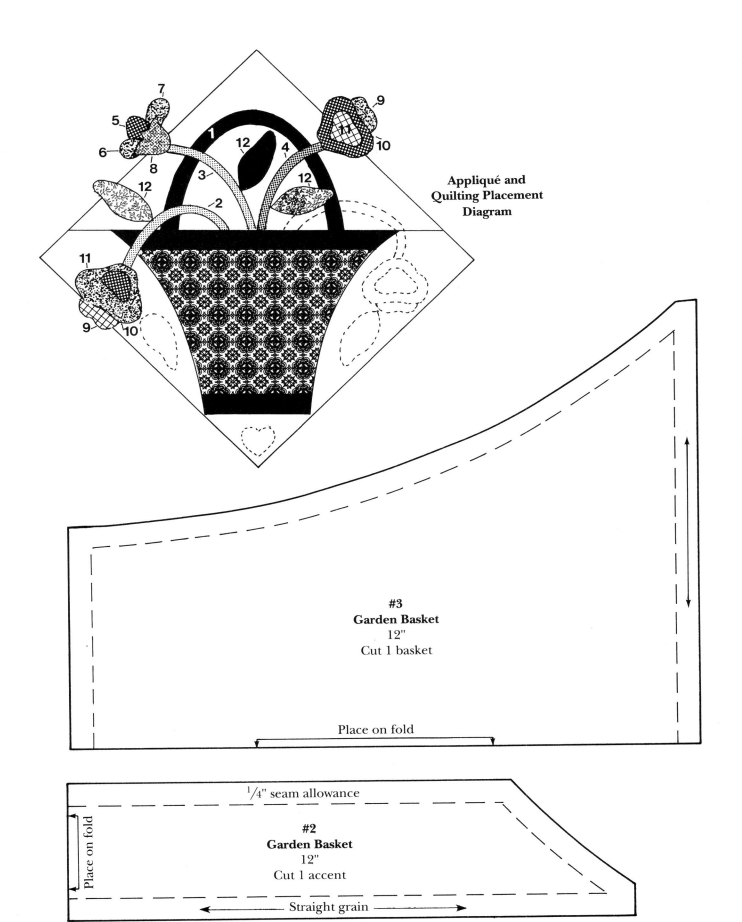

**Appliqué and
Quilting Placement
Diagram**

**#3
Garden Basket
12"
Cut 1 basket**

Place on fold

$^1/_4$" seam allowance

Place on fold

**#2
Garden Basket
12"
Cut 1 accent**

Straight grain

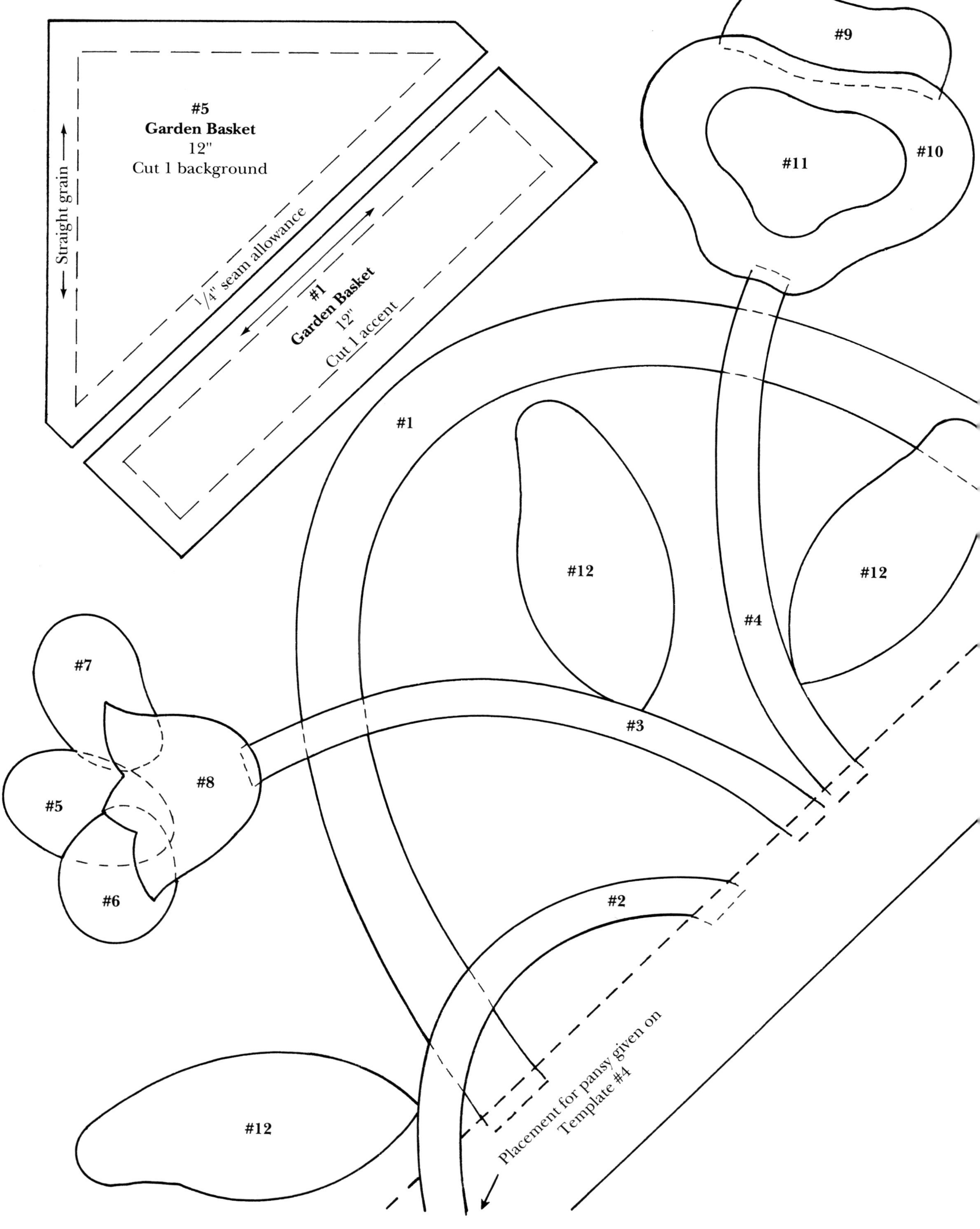

#9

#11 #10

#5
Garden Basket
12"
Cut 1 background

Straight grain

¹/₄" seam allowance

#1
Garden Basket
12"
Cut 1 accent

#1

#12

#12

#4

#7

#3

#8

#5

#12

#6

#2

Placement for pansy given on
Template #4

#12

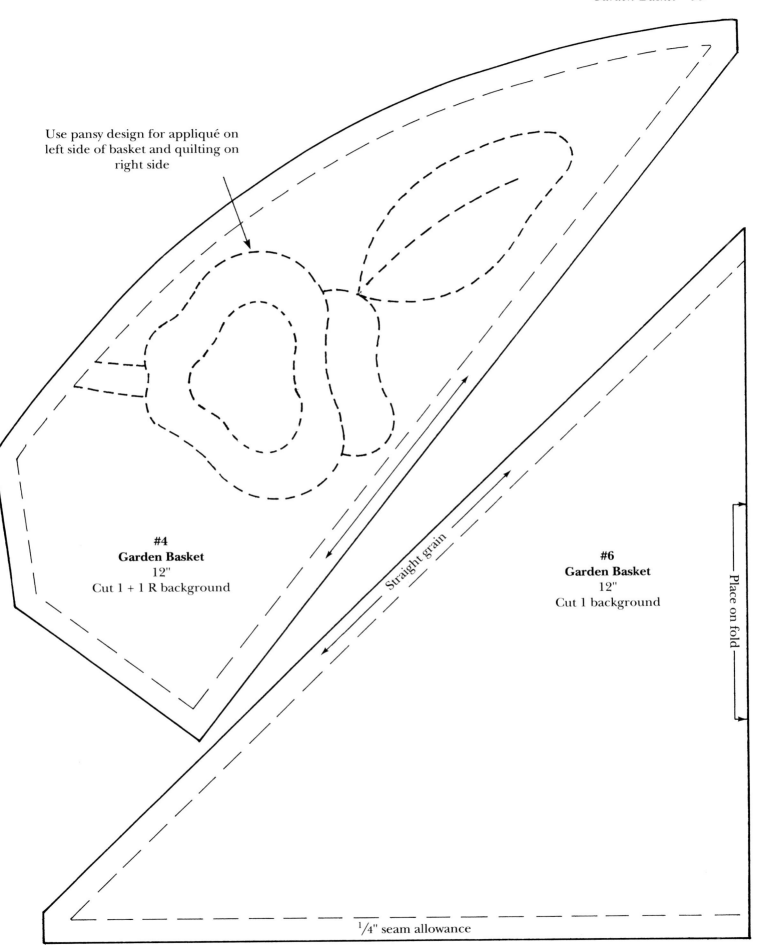

Use pansy design for appliqué on left side of basket and quilting on right side

#4
Garden Basket
12"
Cut 1 + 1 R background

Straight grain

#6
Garden Basket
12"
Cut 1 background

Place on fold

$^1/4$" seam allowance

Victorian Basket

The interlaced handle and flowing curves of the Victorian Basket are reminiscent of a more graceful era. Its blooming flowers make it especially appropriate for a spring wall hanging. The construction is simple and fast.

Materials: (44"–45" wide fabric)

$^3/_8$ yd. fabric for background
$^1/_4$ yd. fabric for basket
$^1/_8$ yd. each or scraps of 4 fabrics for leaves and flowers
$^1/_3$ yd. fabric for set triangles

Templates

#1–#3, pages 57–58
Background template #4 on pull-out pattern page
Set Triangle template on pull-out pattern page

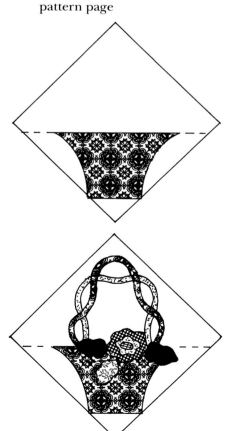

DIRECTIONS

1. Arrange the pieces on your work surface to form the block.

2. Pin thin background side pieces (Template #2) to the basket (Template #1). Pin the top, bottom, and center; then, put in several more pins to ease the pieces together.

 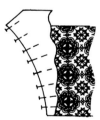

3. Stitch the pieces with the background on top. Press toward the basket.

4. Stitch the top triangle (Template #4) and bottom triangle (Template #3) to the basket.

5. Sew the set triangles to the basket block.

6. Cut 2 bias strips of basket fabric, each 1" x 18"; appliqué the handles.

7. Appliqué the flower and leaves.

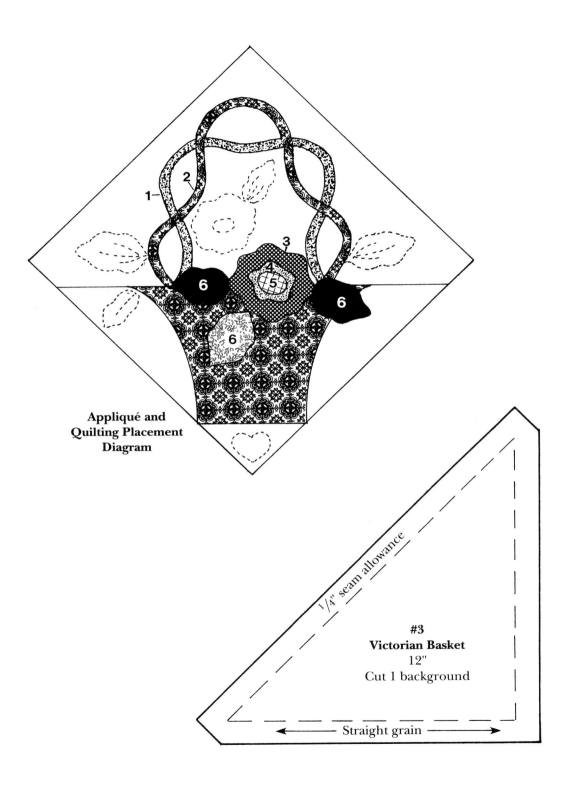

**Appliqué and
Quilting Placement
Diagram**

¼" seam allowance

**#3
Victorian Basket**
12"
Cut 1 background

Straight grain

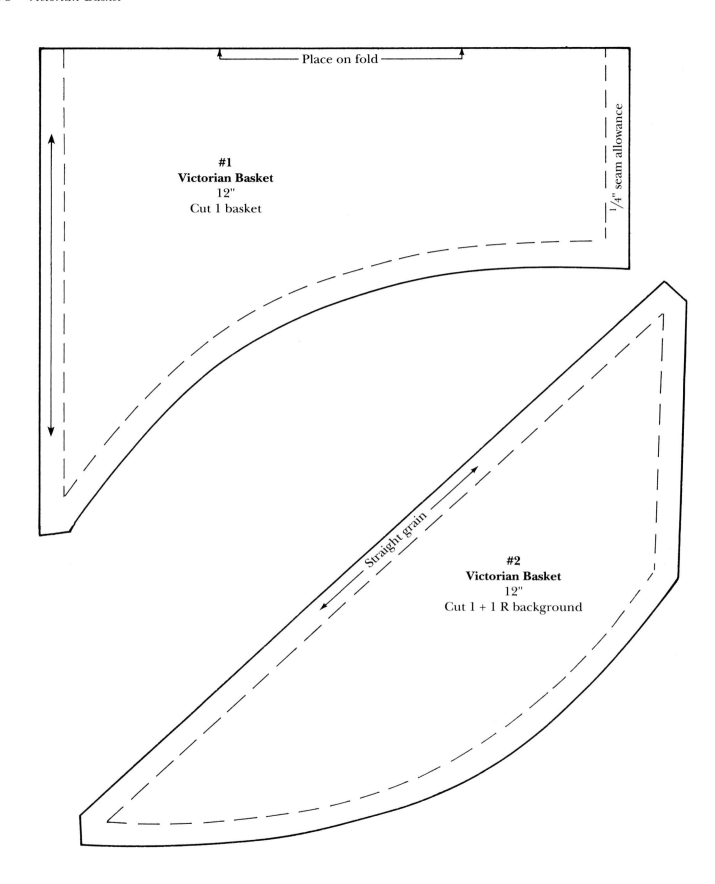

Place on fold

¹/₄" seam allowance

#1
Victorian Basket
12"
Cut 1 basket

Straight grain

#2
Victorian Basket
12"
Cut 1 + 1 R background

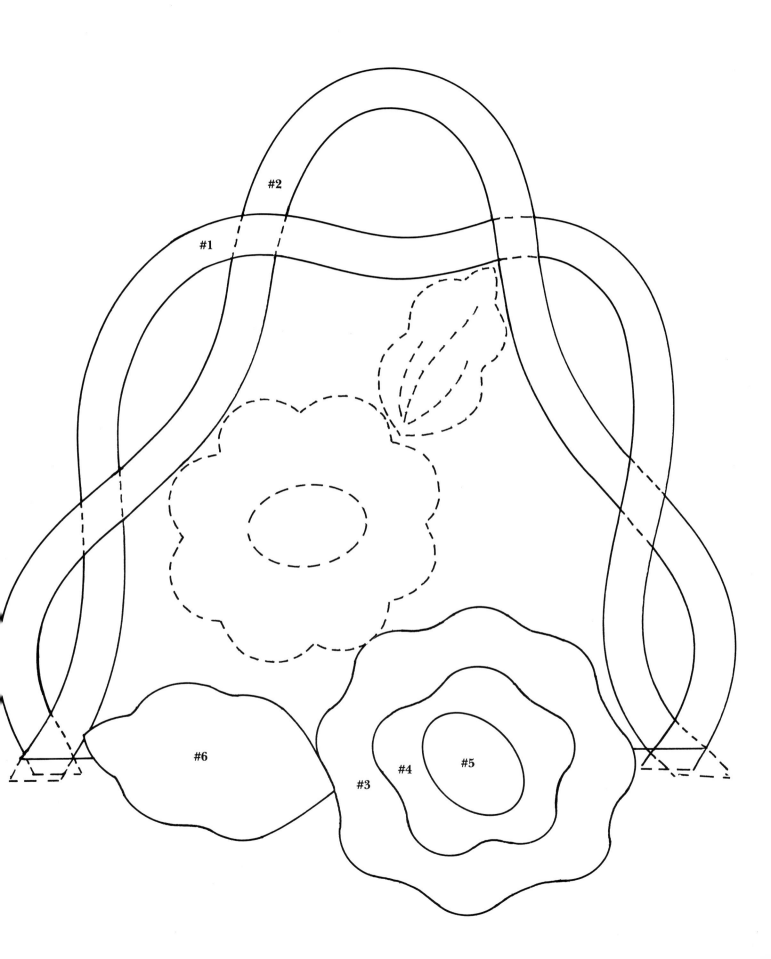

#1

#2

#3

#4

#5

#6

Peony Basket

The peony, exuberant in its colors and extravagant in its fragrance, is fascinating to piece. This basket pattern is an adaptation of the traditional Duck Paddle pattern. The colors can be varied to change it to a Poinsettia for a Christmas wall hanging (see page 85).

Materials: (44"–45" wide fabric)

³/₈ yd. fabric for background
¹/₄ yd. fabric for basket
¹/₈ yd. each or scraps of 5 fabrics for peonies, stems, and leaves
¹/₃ yd. fabric for set triangles

Templates

#1–#11, pages 61–63
Set Triangle template on pull-out pattern page

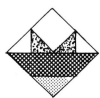

DIRECTIONS FOR PEONIES

1. Arrange all pieces on your work surface to form the block.

2. Make 3 units with the small peony triangle (Template #1) on the right.

3. Make 3 units with the small peony triangle (Template #1) on the left.

4. Stitch a small background square (Template #2) to the peony-on-the-right units.

5. Sew a peony-on-the-left unit to the other side of each square.

6. Sew a medium-sized peony triangle (Template #4) to each trapezoid (Template #3).

7. Sew a trapezoid unit to each triangle unit to create the peony.

8. Arrange the peony units, turning them in the proper direction, as illustrated.

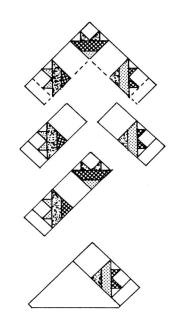

9. Stitch a background rectangle (Template #6) and a square (Template #5) to 2 of the peony blossoms.

10. Sew the remaining peony to 1 of the peony units made in step 9.

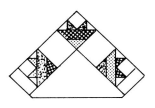

11. Sew the smaller of these units to the large background triangle (Template #7). Press toward the peony.

12. Stitch the two-peony unit to the large unit made in step 11. Press toward the peonies.

DIRECTIONS FOR BASKET

1. Sew the small basket triangle (Template #9) to the background trapezoids (Template #8).

2. Stitch the trapezoid units to the basket triangle (Template #10).

3. Sew the small background triangle (Template #11) to the bottom of the basket unit.

4. Sew the basket section to the blossom section.

5. Attach the set triangles.

6. Appliqué the stems, using 3 bias strips, each 1" x 8". Open seams and tuck in ends of stems.

7. Appliqué the leaves.

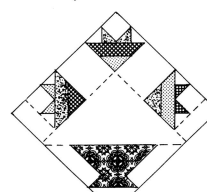

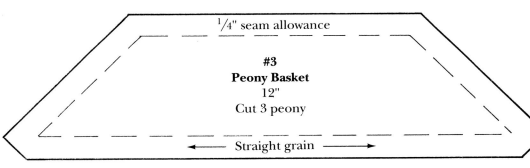

¹/4" seam allowance

#3
Peony Basket
12"
Cut 3 peony

← Straight grain →

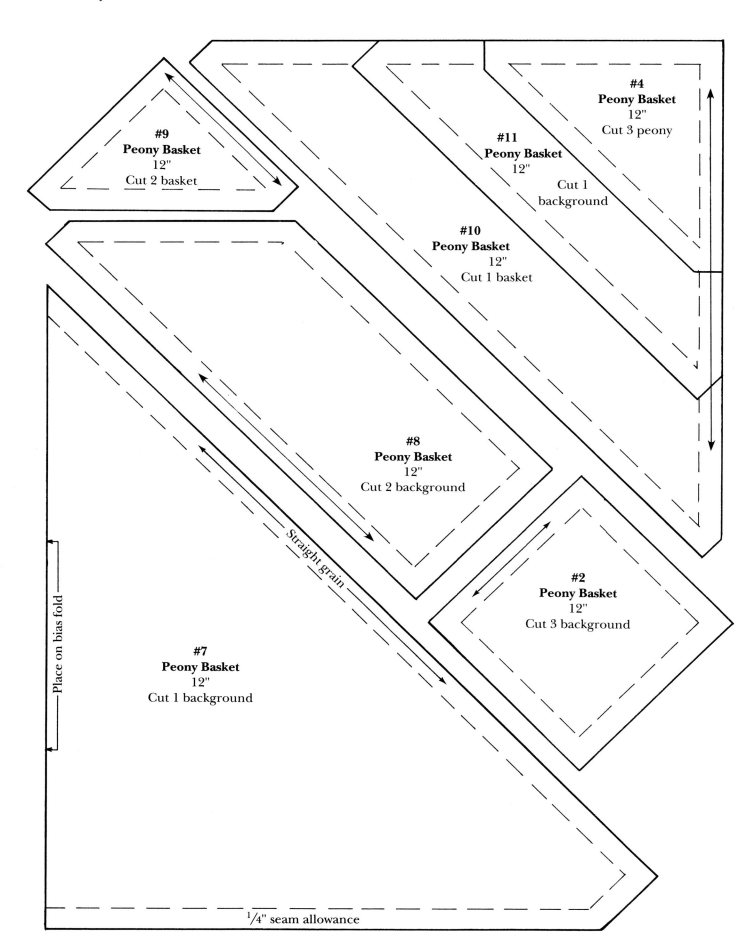

#9
Peony Basket
12"
Cut 2 basket

#11
Peony Basket
12"
Cut 1
background

#4
Peony Basket
12"
Cut 3 peony

#10
Peony Basket
12"
Cut 1 basket

#8
Peony Basket
12"
Cut 2 background

Straight grain

Place on bias fold

#7
Peony Basket
12"
Cut 1 background

#2
Peony Basket
12"
Cut 3 background

¼" seam allowance

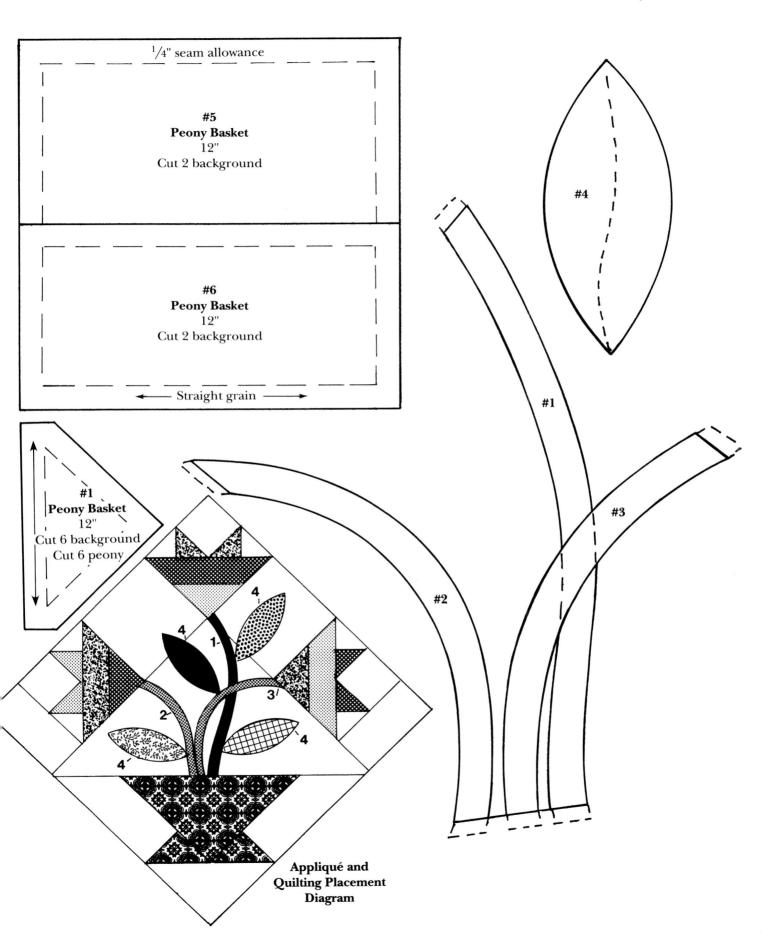

¹/₄" seam allowance

#5
Peony Basket
12"
Cut 2 background

#6
Peony Basket
12"
Cut 2 background

←——— Straight grain ———→

#1
Peony Basket
12"
Cut 6 background
Cut 6 peony

#4

#1

#3

#2

Appliqué and
Quilting Placement
Diagram

Tulip Basket

Pioneer women grew tulips in their gardens and used fabric to piece them into their quilt tops. The vivacious Tulip Basket is endearing in its simplicity and intriguing in its construction.

Materials: (44"–45" wide fabric)

¼ yd. fabric for background
¼ yd. fabric for basket
⅛ yd. each or scraps of 3 fabrics, including a dark and a medium, for tulips
⅛ yd. each or scraps of 2 fabrics for stems and leaves
⅓ yd. fabric for set triangles

Templates

#1–#9, pages 65–67
Set Triangle template on pull-out pattern page

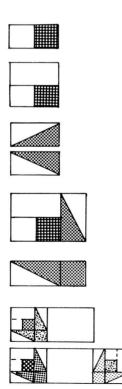

DIRECTIONS FOR TULIPS

1. Arrange all pieces on your work surface to form the block.

2. Sew 3 units of the medium-colored fabric squares and background squares (Template #1).

3. Add a background rectangle (Template #2) to each square unit.

4. Stitch 6 units of dark and background triangles (Template #3). The units will form a rectangle. You will have 3 pairs of mirror images.

5. Sew a triangle unit to the square unit. Be sure the dark color touches the medium-colored square. Make 3 of these units. Press toward the triangles.

6. Sew a dark square (Template #1) to the base of each remaining triangle unit. Be sure the darks touch each other. Make 3 of these units. Press toward the triangles.

7. Assemble the 3 tulips.

8. Stitch 1 large background rectangle (Template #4) to a tulip unit and the other large rectangle (Template #4) between 2 tulips. Be sure the tulips are facing the proper way.

9. Sew the large background triangle (Template #5) to the one-tulip unit. Press toward the tulip.

10. Sew the two-tulip unit to the unit made in step 9.

DIRECTIONS FOR BASKET

1. Stitch the 2 small basket triangles (Template #7) to the long background trapezoids (Template #6).

2. Stitch the trapezoid units to the basket triangle (Template #10).

3. Sew the small background triangle (Template #11) to the bottom of the basket unit.

4. Stitch the basket section to the peony section.

5. Sew the set triangles to the block.

6. Appliqué the stems, using 3 bias strips, each 1" x 8". Open seams and tuck in ends of stems.

7. Appliqué the leaves.

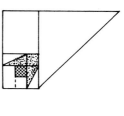
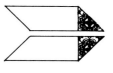

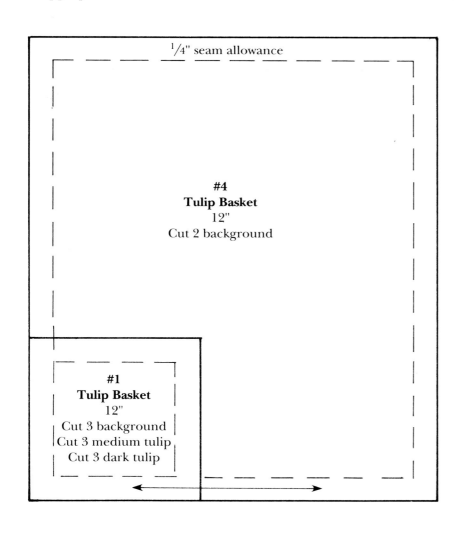

¼" seam allowance

#4
Tulip Basket
12"
Cut 2 background

#1
Tulip Basket
12"
Cut 3 background
Cut 3 medium tulip
Cut 3 dark tulip

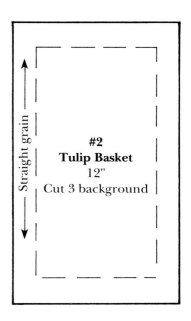

Straight grain

#2
Tulip Basket
12"
Cut 3 background

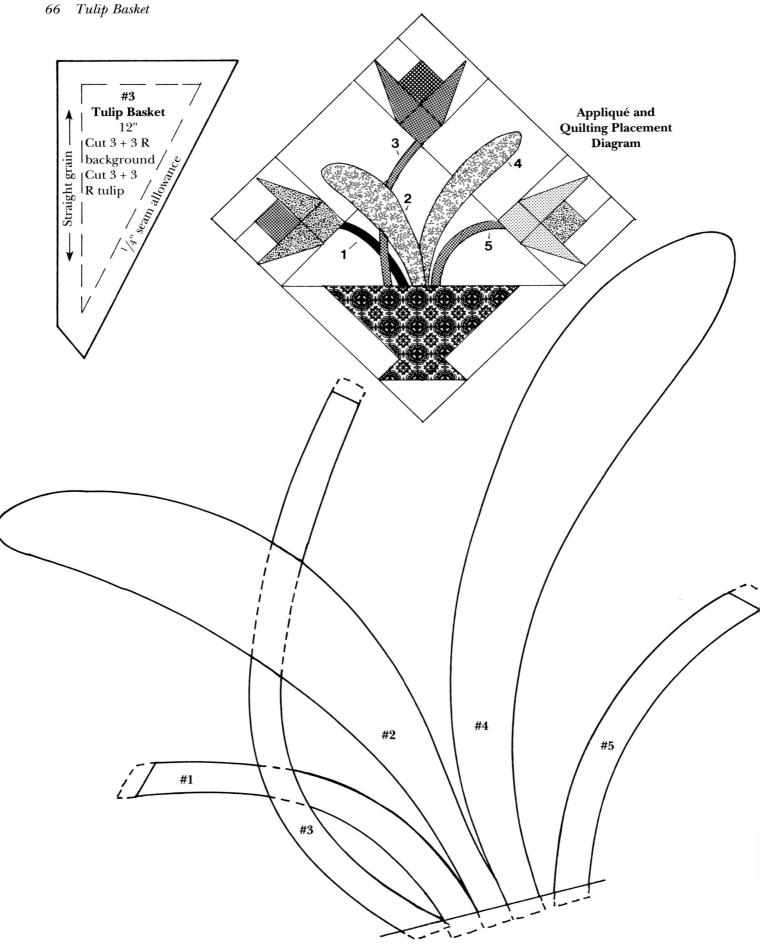

#3
Tulip Basket
12"
Cut 3 + 3 R background
Cut 3 + 3 R tulip

Straight grain

1/4" seam allowance

Appliqué and Quilting Placement Diagram

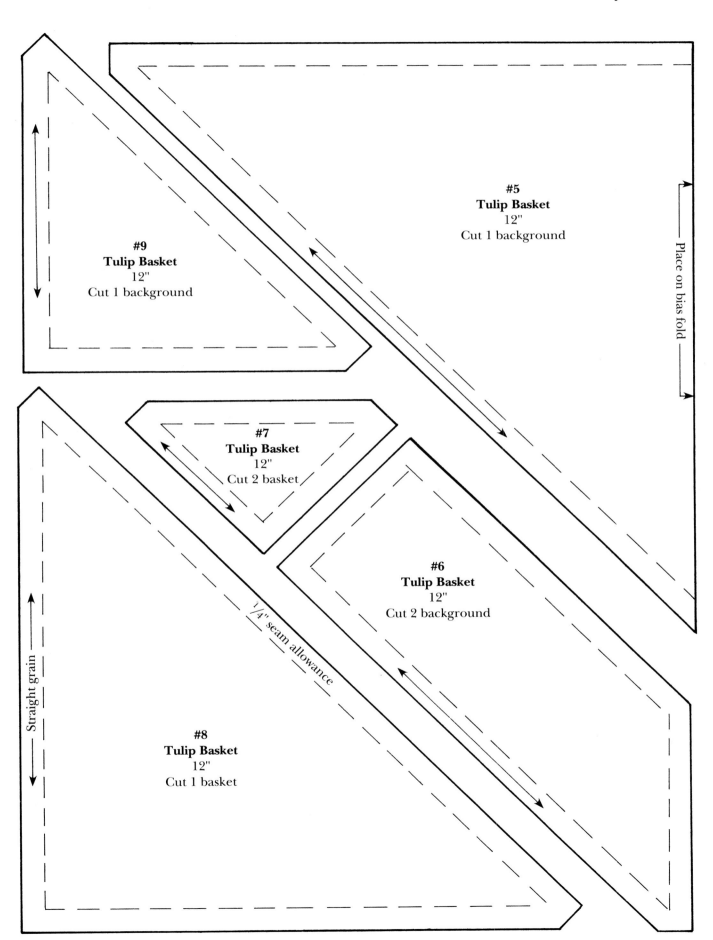

#5
Tulip Basket
12"
Cut 1 background

Place on bias fold

#9
Tulip Basket
12"
Cut 1 background

#7
Tulip Basket
12"
Cut 2 basket

#6
Tulip Basket
12"
Cut 2 background

1/4" seam allowance

Straight grain

#8
Tulip Basket
12"
Cut 1 basket

Daffodil Basket

The sight of daffodils dancing in the chilly March winds reminds us that spring is near. Because the petals fit together like puzzle pieces, these cheerful flowers are interesting to piece.

Materials: (44"–45" wide fabric)

¹/₄ yd. fabric for background
¹/₄ yd. fabric for basket
¹/₈ yd. each or scraps of 4 fabrics for flowers, stems, and leaves
¹/₃ yd. fabric for set triangles

Templates

#1–#11, pages 69–71
Set Triangle template on pull-out pattern page

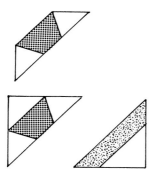

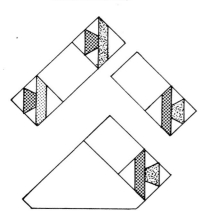

DIRECTIONS FOR DAFFODILS

1. Arrange the pieces on your work surface to form the block.

2. Sew 2 triangles (Template #2) to either side of trapezoid (Template #1). When the 3 pieces are arranged together, they form a straight line across the bottom.

3. Sew small triangle (Template #3) to top of unit made in step 2.

4. Stitch Template #4 to Template #5.

5. Sew templates #1–2–3 to templates #4–5, creating the daffodil. Make 3 of these units.

6. Stitch a background rectangle (Template #6) between 2 of the daffodils.

7. Sew the other background rectangle (Template #6) to the remaining daffodil and sew the large background triangle (Template #7) to this unit.

8. Sew the two-daffodil unit from step 6 to the triangle-daffodil unit.

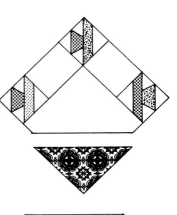

DIRECTIONS FOR BASKET

1. Stitch the large basket triangle (Template #8) to the daffodil section.

2. Sew the small basket triangles (Template #10) to the long background rectangle (Template #9).

3. Stitch these to the basket-daffodil unit.

4. Sew the background triangle (Template #11) to the base of the basket to complete the block.

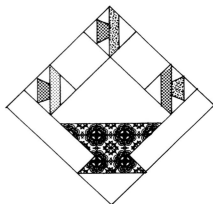

5. Stitch the set triangles to the block.

6. Appliqué the stems, using 3 bias strips, each 1" x 8". Open seams and tuck in ends of stems.

7. Appliqué the leaves.

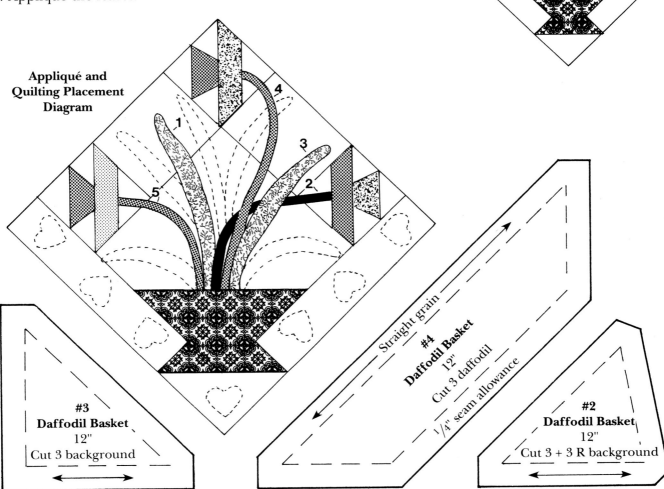

Appliqué and Quilting Placement Diagram

#3
Daffodil Basket
12"
Cut 3 background

Straight grain
#4
Daffodil Basket
12"
Cut 3 daffodil
1/4" seam allowance

#2
Daffodil Basket
12"
Cut 3 + 3 R background

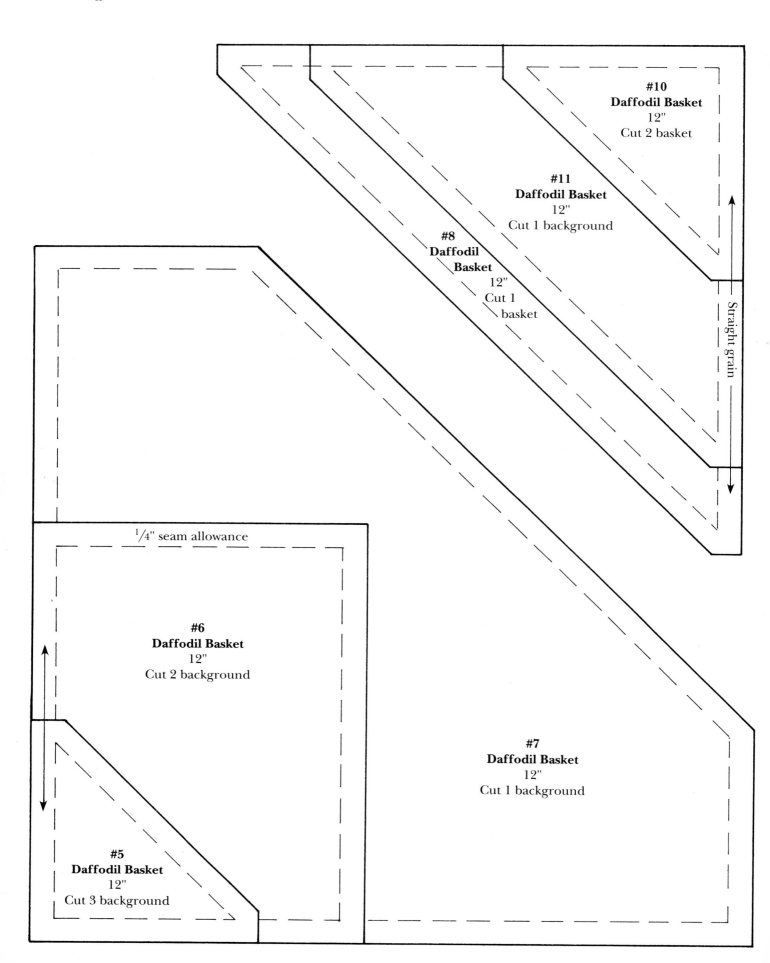

#10
Daffodil Basket
12"
Cut 2 basket

#11
Daffodil Basket
12"
Cut 1 background

#8
Daffodil Basket
12"
Cut 1 basket

Straight grain

¼" seam allowance

#6
Daffodil Basket
12"
Cut 2 background

#7
Daffodil Basket
12"
Cut 1 background

#5
Daffodil Basket
12"
Cut 3 background

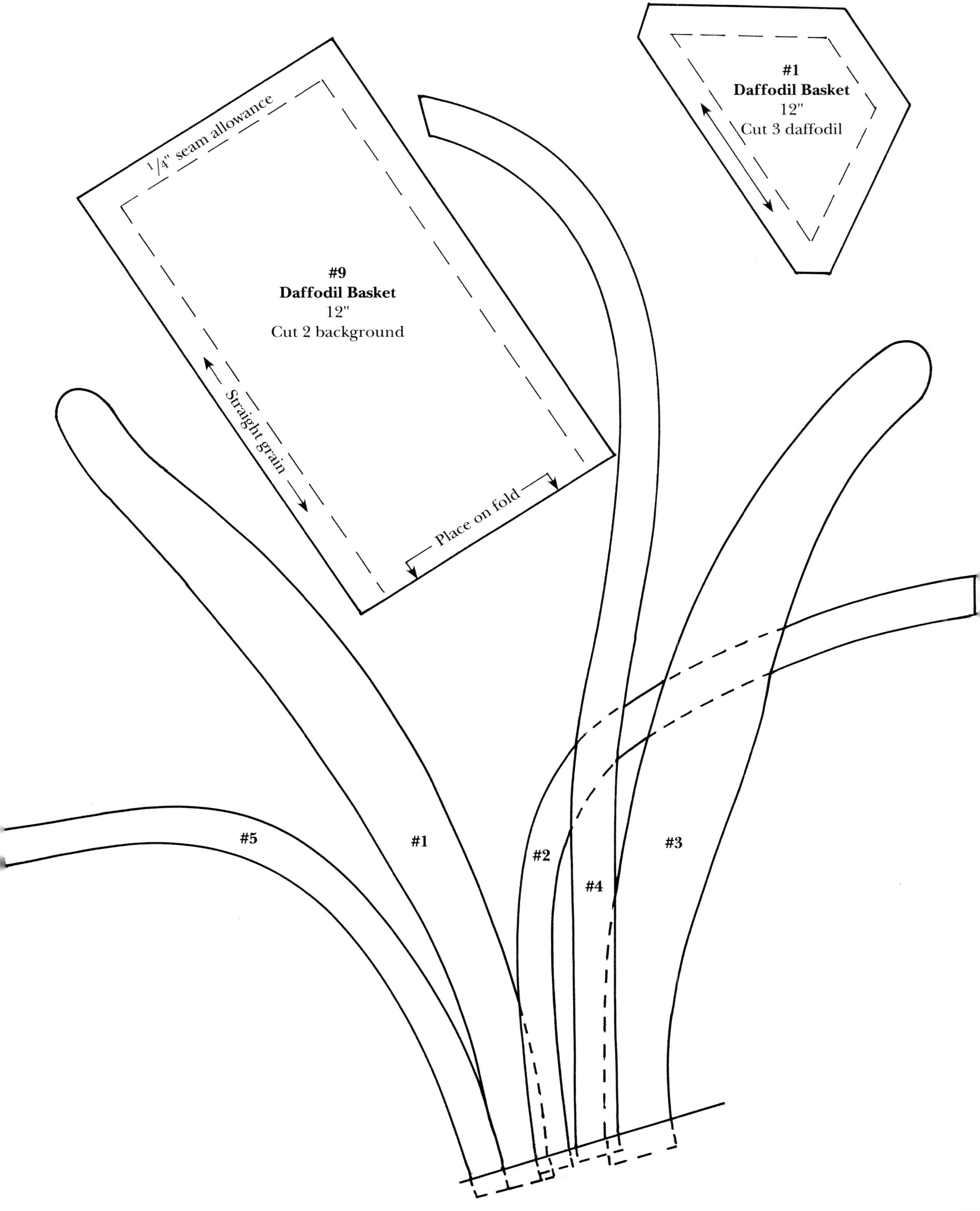

#1
Daffodil Basket
12"
Cut 3 daffodil

¼" seam allowance

#9
Daffodil Basket
12"
Cut 2 background

Straight grain

Place on fold

#5

#1

#2

#4

#3

Quilt Patterns

Five complete quilt plans are given for quilts made with all or various combinations of basket blocks. Each quilt pattern will refer you to the appropriate basket block directions. Consult the Glossary of Techniques on pages 90–91 for complete instructions on finishing your quilt.

Swinging on the Garden Gate

81" x 96"

An old-fashioned garden, populated by an array of vividly colored flowers and neatly enclosed by a white picket fence, gives this quilt an innocent, almost naive gaiety. Since the flower colors vary from block to block, the greens of the baskets, foliage, and border remain constant to give the quilt a straightforward, cheerful unity.

Materials: (44"–45" wide fabric)

3 yds. fabric for background
1^1/$_2$ yds. fabric for main basket
^{1}/$_2$ yd. for alternate basket
^{1}/$_4$ yd. or scraps of each of 12 different fabrics for flowers, stems, leaves, hearts, birds, and ribbons
3^3/$_4$ yds. fabric for border (green)
1^1/$_4$ yds. fabric for pickets (white)
6 yds. fabric for backing
Batting, binding, and thread to finish

Templates

Templates for all the blocks in the Heirloom Basket Sampler #1–#7, page 75

DIRECTIONS FOR QUILT

1. Cut fabrics for blocks as directed on templates.

2. Piece the baskets according to the instructions for each block.

3. Sew the set triangles to the basket block.

4. Appliqué the shapes as directed on templates.

5. Join the blocks into rows.

6. Sew the rows together to create the quilt top.

DIRECTIONS FOR BORDER

1. Cut the following:

   Green: 8 strips, each 4^1/$_2$" x 44"
   12 strips, each 3^1/$_2$" x 44"
   4 strips, each 2^1/$_2$" x 44"
   4 strips, each 2" x 44"
   2 pieces, each 4^1/$_2$" x 9"
   2 pieces, each 4^1/$_2$" x 13^1/$_2$"

   White: 13 strips, each 2^1/$_2$" x 44" (Cut these strips into 56 rectangles, each 2^1/$_2$" x 8", for pickets)
   6 strips, each 1^1/$_2$" x 44"

2. Stitch 56 triangle units.

3. Sew a triangle unit to each white rectangle to create the pickets.

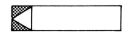

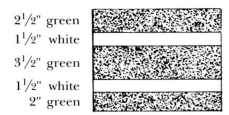

2¹/₂" green
1¹/₂" white
3¹/₂" green
1¹/₂" white
2" green

4. Stitch 3 identical units according to the diagram to create the rail units. Press toward the green.

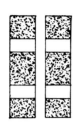

5. Cut across the rail units at 2¹/₂" intervals to create the rails.

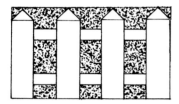

6. Sew the rails between the pickets in 2 groups of 18 pickets and 1 group of 20 pickets.

7. Sew 8 of the 3¹/₂" wide strips together end to end in pairs. Sew 8 of the 4¹/₂" wide strips together end to end in pairs.

8. Stitch 3¹/₂" wide pairs of strips to the side of the quilt; trim.

9. Stitch 3¹/₂" wide pairs of strips to the top and bottom of the quilt; trim.

10. Sew a 4¹/₂" x 9" piece of green to the ends of the 18 picket sets. These should be sewn to ends that will be on the bottom of the quilt.

11. Stitch 4¹/₂" pairs of strips on the outside of the 18 picket units.

12. Stitch the 18 picket units to the sides of the quilt.

13. Sew a 4¹/₂" x 13¹/₂" piece of green to the ends of the 20-picket unit.

14. Sew the 20-picket unit to the bottom of the quilt.

15. Stitch 4¹/₂" pairs of strips to the top and bottom of the quilt.

16. Baste the quilt top to the batting and backing; then quilt.

17. Bind with bias strips.

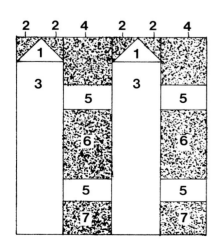

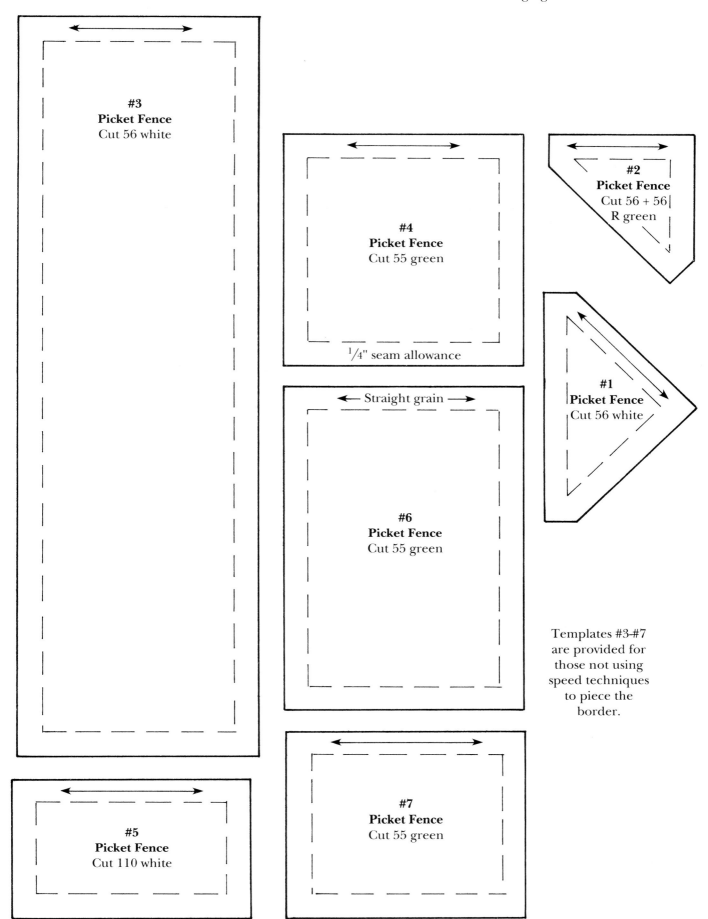

#3
Picket Fence
Cut 56 white

#4
Picket Fence
Cut 55 green

$1/4$" seam allowance

#2
Picket Fence
Cut 56 + 56
R green

#1
Picket Fence
Cut 56 white

Straight grain

#6
Picket Fence
Cut 55 green

Templates #3-#7
are provided for
those not using
speed techniques
to piece the
border.

#5
Picket Fence
Cut 110 white

#7
Picket Fence
Cut 55 green

Bandana Baskets

76" x 96"

Memories of summer days spent visiting our cousins' farm in central Illinois are celebrated in this quilt. Baskets for gathering vegetables and collecting eggs are the inspiration for these blocks stitched in the colors of denim jeans, plaid shirts, and red bandanas. The baskets are a breeze to piece, and the handles and bows are easy to appliqué.

Materials: (44"–45" wide fabric)

$1\frac{1}{2}$ yds. fabric for background
6 yds. fabric for settings and borders
1 yd. fabric for border squares
$\frac{1}{4}$ yd. each or large scraps of 16 fabrics for baskets
$\frac{1}{8}$ yd. each or scraps of 12 fabrics for ribbons
$5\frac{1}{2}$ yds. fabric for backing
Batting, binding, and thread to finish

Templates

Farm Basket, pages 34–35
Market Basket, pages 45–47
Background and Set Triangle templates on pull-out pattern pages
Appliqué ribbon templates for Ribbon Basket, page 31
Border templates #1–#4, pages 78–79 (if not using Seminole technique to piece border)

DIRECTIONS

1. Cut 4 strips, 5" x 98", and 4 strips, 5" x 78", for borders.

2. Cut six $12\frac{1}{2}$" squares for set blocks.

3. Cut two 10" squares. Cut each square in half on the diagonal, creating a total of 4 triangles. These will be the corners of the setting.

4. Cut three $18\frac{1}{2}$" squares. Draw diagonal lines across the squares, creating 4 triangles from each square. Cut on these lines to make the side, top, and bottom triangles of the setting.

5. Cut fabrics for the pieced section of the border as directed on the templates. You can make the pieced section of the border by using the Seminole technique described in steps 2–6 of the Market Basket pattern on page 44. Cut strips and segments $3\frac{1}{2}$" wide. Cut 12 of dark fabric and 6 of light fabric. The time saved by using the Seminole method compensates for the small amount of fabric that is wasted.

6. Cut fabrics for the 12 baskets and ribbons as directed on the templates. Cut $1\frac{1}{2}$" x 18" bias strips for handles on each of the baskets.

7. Piece the baskets according to the instructions for each block (see page 32 for Farm Basket and page 44 for Market Basket).

8. Appliqué the handles.

9. Arrange the baskets with the set pieces.

10. Stitch the set piece to the upper edge of each Farm Basket.

11. Appliqué the ribbons to the Farm Baskets.

12. Sew the remaining set pieces together with the basket blocks in diagonal rows. Join rows to create the quilt top.

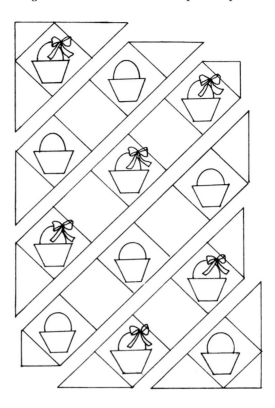

13. Sew together the pieced sections of the border, following the diagram on page 79.

14. Sew borders to quilt top, mitering the corners.

15. Baste the quilt top to the batting and backing; then quilt.

16. Bind with bias strips.

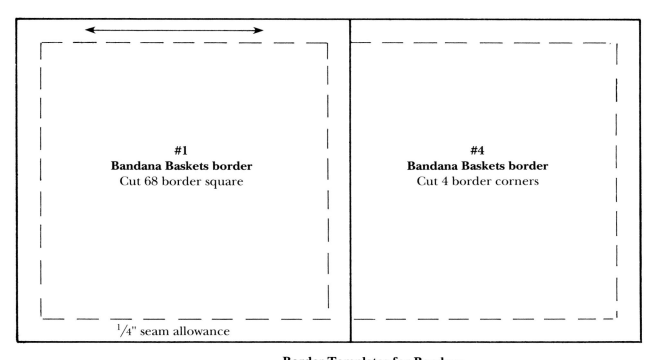

#1
Bandana Baskets border
Cut 68 border square

#4
Bandana Baskets border
Cut 4 border corners

¹/₄" seam allowance

**Border Templates for Bandana
Baskets**
(if not using Seminole technique
to piece border)

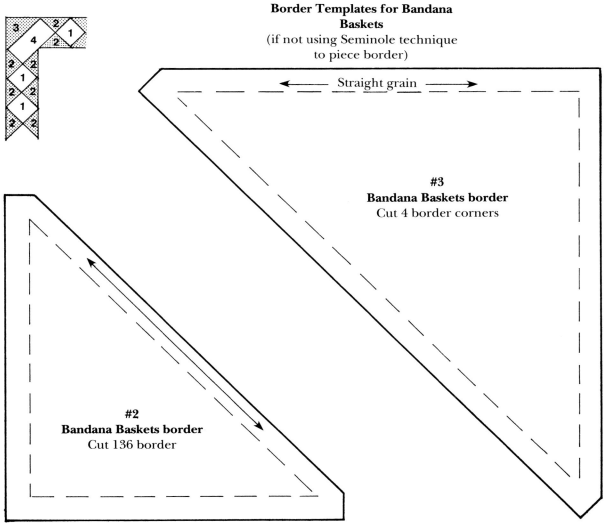

Straight grain

#3
Bandana Baskets border
Cut 4 border corners

#2
Bandana Baskets border
Cut 136 border

Tear along the Dotted Line

80" x 93"

Tiny Stamp Baskets, sashed with narrow strips, radiate energy across the surface of this quilt. The secondary patterns that emerge between the blocks add interest and vitality. The baskets are easy to piece and the handles are quick to appliqué.

Materials: (44"–45" wide fabric)

4 yds. fabric for background
$^{1}/_{8}$ yd. each or scraps of 24 different fabrics for baskets
$^{3}/_{4}$ yd. fabric for inner border
1 yd. green fabric for sashing
2$^{1}/_{2}$ yds. chintz fabric for outer border
5$^{1}/_{8}$ yds. fabric for backing
Batting, binding, and thread to finish

Templates

Stamp Basket, pages 42–43
Set Triangle template on pull-out pattern page

DIRECTIONS FOR BLOCKS

1. Cut background for 20 blocks as directed on templates.

2. Cut baskets from a variety of prints as directed on templates. (Fabrics can be stacked and several pieces cut at once.)

3. Cut a 1" x 7" bias strip from each basket fabric for handles.

4. Sew bias strips for handles.

5. Using Template #1 as a guide, pin handles to the center square of each block. (Machine basting the handles to the square will make it easier to appliqué them.)

6. Appliqué the handles.

7. Piece the blocks according to the instructions for Stamp Basket on page 40.

DIRECTIONS FOR SASHING AND BORDERS

1. Cut 2 strips of background fabric, each $^{3}/_{4}$" x 22". Cut 5 strips of background fabric, each 1$^{1}/_{2}$" x 22". Cut 6 strips of green fabric, each 1$^{1}/_{2}$" x 22".

2. Stitch the strips together, alternating the colors. The $^{3}/_{4}$" wide strips should be sewn on the outsides of the unit.

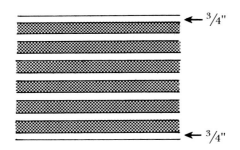

3. Cut across the sewn strips at 1$^{1}/_{4}$" intervals, creating 15 sashing units.

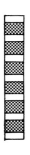

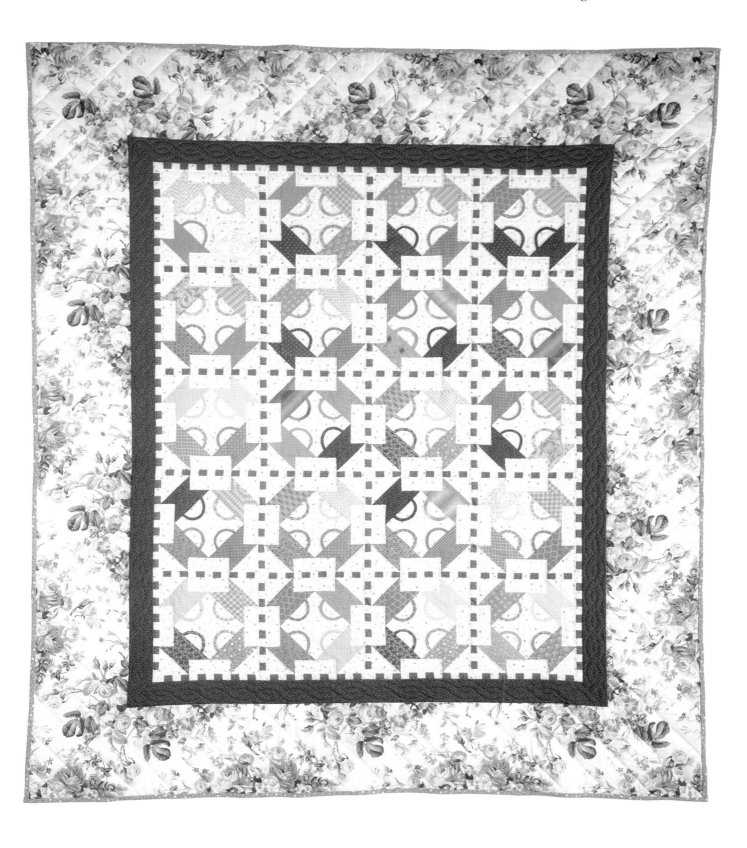

4. Stitch the sashing pieces between the blocks, creating 5 rows of blocks.

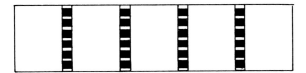

5. Cut 1 strip of background fabric 2½" x 45". Cut 5 strips of background fabric 1½" x 45". Cut 6 strips of green fabric 1½" x 45".

6. Stitch the strips together, alternating the fabrics. Sew the 2½" wide strip on the outside edge of the unit.

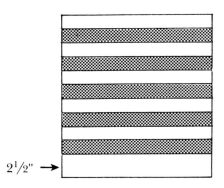

2½" ➜

7. Cut across the sewn strips at 1¼" intervals, creating 34 sashing pieces.

8. Sew the ends of 24 of the sashing pieces together in groups of 4 to create 6 long strips of sashing.

9. Stitch the long pieces of sashing between the rows of blocks to create the quilt top. Stitch sashing pieces to the top and bottom of the quilt top.

10. Sew the ends of 10 of the sashing pieces together in groups of 5 to create 2 long strips of sashing. Sew these to the sides of the quilt top.

11. Cut 2 strips, 3" x 66", from inner border fabric. Cut 2 strips, 3" x 53", from inner border fabric.

12. Cut 2 strips of chintz, 12" x 93", for outer border. Cut 2 strips of chintz, 12" x 80", for outer border.

13. Stitch borders to quilt top, mitering the corners.

14. Baste the quilt top to the batting and backing; then quilt.

15. Bind with bias strips.

Gift Baskets

51" x 51"

**Ribbons, hearts, holly, fruit, and
flowers are the gifts bestowed in
these five baskets. Sewn in vibrant
reds and greens, they create a lovely
Christmas wall hanging.**

Materials: (44"–45" wide fabric)

1³/₄ yds. fabric for background
¹/₂ yd. green for baskets
¹/₄ yd. red for baskets and borders
¹/₄ yd. print for baskets
¹/₈ yd. each or scraps of 3 fabrics for
    ribbons, fruit, flowers, stems,
    and leaves
¹/₂ yd. fabric for sashing
¹/₄ yd. fabric for inner border
¹/₂ yd. fabric for outer border
1¹/₂ yds. fabric for backing
Batting, binding, and thread to
    finish

Templates

Ribbon Basket, page 30
County Fair Basket, pages 38–39
Peony Basket, pages 61–63
Harvest Basket, pages 49–51
Cherry Basket, page 26
Background templates on pages 27,
    38, 62, and on pull-out pattern
    page
#1–#4, pages 86–87 and on pull-out
    pattern pages

DIRECTIONS FOR BLOCKS

1. Cut pieces for baskets as instructed on templates.

2. Piece the baskets according to the instructions for each block (see page 28 for Ribbon Basket, page 36 for County Fair Basket, page 60 for Peony Basket, page 48 for Harvest Basket, and page 24 for Cherry Basket.

3. Cut appliqué shapes as directed on templates.

4. Appliqué shapes to each block as directed.

DIRECTIONS FOR SASHING

1. Cut 2 strips, each 2¹/₄" x 44".
   Cut 8 strips, each 2¹/₄" x 16".
   Cut 6 strips, each 2¹/₄" x 12¹/₂".

2. Stitch the 2¹/₄" x 12¹/₂" strips between 3 of the basket blocks.

3. Sew the 44" strips to the long sides of the three–block unit and stitch two of the 16" strips to the ends of the unit and miter the corners (see page 90).

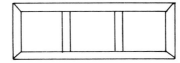

4. Sew the 16" strips to the upper left and lower right of the Cherry Baskets and County Fair Baskets.

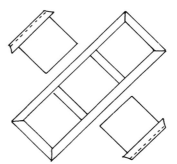

5. Stitch the 16" strips to the outside edge of each basket.

6. Miter all corners.

7. Cut set piece triangles as instructed on templates #1 and #2, pages 86–87.

8. Cut inner border pieces as instructed on templates #3 and #4 on pull-out pattern pages.

9. Sew inner border pieces to set pieces.

 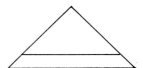

10. Arrange set pieces with blocks in diagonal rows.

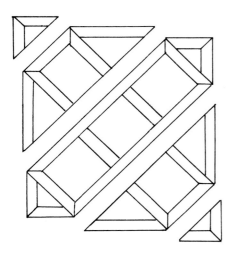

11. Stitch together into quilt top.

12. Cut 4 outer border strips, each 5" x 51".

13. Sew borders to quilt top, mitering the corners.

14. Baste the quilt top to the batting and backing; then quilt.

15. Bind with bias strips.

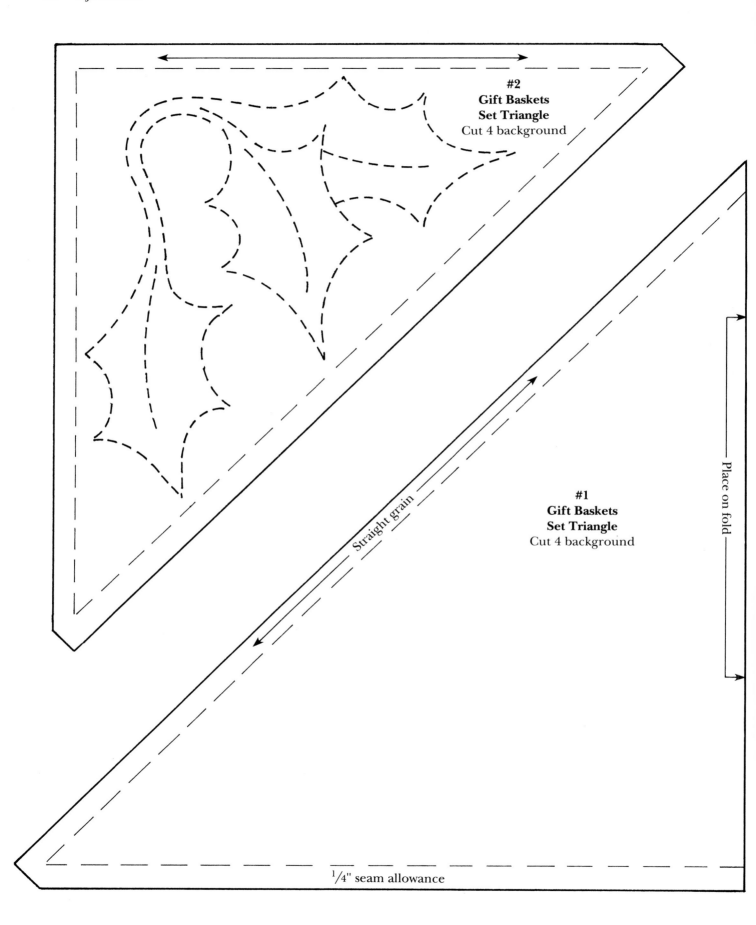

#2
Gift Baskets
Set Triangle
Cut 4 background

#1
Gift Baskets
Set Triangle
Cut 4 background

Straight grain

Place on fold

¹/4" seam allowance

#5

#4

#3

#2

#1

Quilting design for set piece

Spring Baskets

41" x 41"

Two baskets filled with pieced flowers, combined with two classic curved baskets, create a lovely spring wall hanging. The appliqué is simple, yet it adds grace to the crisp flowers.

Materials: (44"–45" wide fabric)

$^3/_4$ yd. fabric for background
$^7/_8$ yd. fabric for setting
$^1/_3$ yd. fabric for baskets
$^1/_8$ yd. each or scraps of 8 fabrics for flowers, ribbons, stems, and leaves
$^1/_4$ yd. fabric for inner border
$^1/_2$ yd. fabric for outer border
$1^1/_4$ yds. fabric for backing
Batting, binding, and thread to finish

Templates

Tulip Basket, pages 65–67
Daffodil Basket, pages 69–71
Garden Basket, pages 53–55
Victorian Basket, pages 57–58
Background and Set Triangle templates on pull-out pattern pages
Ribbon Appliqué template, page 31

DIRECTIONS

1. Cut 4 strips inner border fabric, each $1^1/_4$" x 36".

2. Cut 4 strips of outer border fabric, each $3^1/_2$" x 44".

3. Cut fabrics for blocks as directed on templates.

4. Piece the baskets according to the instructions for each block (see page 64 for Tulip Basket, page 68 for Daffodil Basket, page 52 for Garden Basket, and page 56 for Victorian Basket).

5. Cut appliqué shapes as directed on templates.

6. Appliqué shapes to Tulip, Daffodil, and Victorian blocks.

7. Cut set pieces:
   a. Cut one $12^1/_2$" square.
   b. Cut two 10" squares. Cut each of these squares in half on the diagonal, creating 2 triangles. These are the corners of the setting.

   c. Cut one $18^1/_2$" square. Draw diagonal lines across the square in each direction, creating 4 triangles. Cut on these lines to make the sides, top, and bottom triangles of the setting.

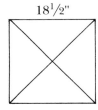

8. Arrange the pieces in diagonal rows.

9. Stitch the set triangle to the upper right side of the Garden Basket.

10. Appliqué the ribbon shapes to the Garden Basket, overlapping part of the ribbon into the set piece.

11. Sew the blocks into the quilt top with the set block and triangles.

12. Stitch borders to quilt top, mitering the corners.

13. Baste the quilt top to the batting and backing; then quilt.

14. Bind with bias strips.

Glossary of Techniques

SETTING BLOCKS TOGETHER

Measure each block to be sure it is square and the same size as the others. If a block is not square, press it carefully, pulling it gently to make it square and trim. Arrange the blocks according to the diagram on page 20 or as you desire. Work in a large area so you can stand back and see how your blocks look. If you have a strong color that dominates one section of the quilt, rearrange the blocks to create a balanced look.

Join the blocks into rows, matching the points. Press the seams in the first and third rows in one direction and the seams in the second and fourth rows in the other direction. Stitch the rows together in groups of two and then four to complete the top. Press the row seams toward the bottom of the quilt.

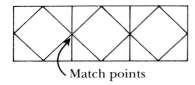

Match points

MITERING CORNERS

1. Measure your quilt top.
2. Calculate the finished outside dimensions of the quilt top.
3. If you are using multiple borders, sew the strips of fabric together, creating striped borders that can be treated as a unit.
4. Center the strips of border fabric on the sides of the quilt top.
5. Start stitching the borders to the quilt top $1/4$" from the end of the quilt and stop $1/4$" from the other end.
6. Stitch the four borders to the quilt, leaving the first and last $1/4$" unsewn.
7. Arrange the quilt with one corner right side up on the ironing board.
8. Fold one border into a 45-degree angle with the other border. Work with the stripes so that they meet.

Arrange the pins with all the heads facing the center of the quilt and press.

9. Use 1" masking tape to tape the mitered angle in place. Start at the outer edge of the quilt and carefully center the tape over the mitered fold as you remove the pins.
10. Turn the quilt over and draw a light pencil line on the crease created by pressing in step 8.
11. Stitch on the pencil line and remove the tape.
12. Repeat steps 7–11 on the remaining three corners.

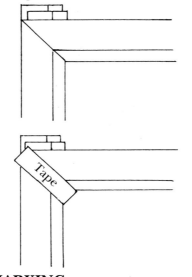

MARKING

Carefully press the quilt top and trace the quilting designs on it. Use a sharp pencil and mark lightly. If you prefer to use a water-soluble pen, test for removability on a scrap before marking the quilt. Chalk dispensers and white pencils are available to mark dark fabrics. The quilt top may be marked for straight-line quilting with $1/4$" masking tape after the quilt is basted.

BACKING

Make a quilt backing that is 2" larger than your quilt top. Trim selvages to avoid puckers and press seams open. Spread the backing wrong side up over a clean, flat surface. Use masking tape to anchor the quilt to the surface without stretching it.

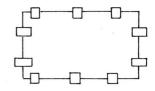

BATTING

Batting is the filler between the backing and the top of the quilt. A lightweight cotton-polyester (80%–20%) combination batting works well. Battings of 100% cotton are also excellent but must be closely quilted to prevent shifting during laundering. Less quilting is needed with a 100% polyester bonded batting. However, some polyester may creep through the fabric and create tiny "beards" on the surface of the quilt. This problem is particularly noticeable on dark fabrics.

BASTING

Spread the quilt batting over the smooth backing, making sure it covers the entire backing and is smooth. Place the pressed and marked top over the batting. Center the quilt right side up over the batting. Align the borders and straight lines with the edges of the backing and pin baste carefully.

Baste the three layers together, using a long needle and light-colored quilting thread. If you thread your needle without cutting the thread off the spool, you will be able to baste at least one long row without rethreading your needle. Starting at the center of the quilt, use large stitches to baste an **X** on the quilt from corner to corner. Continue basting, creating a grid of parallel lines 8"–10" apart. Complete the basting with a line of stitches around the outside edges.

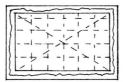

QUILTING

Quilting is simply a short running stitch with a single thread that goes through all three layers of the quilt. Quilt on a frame, a hoop, on a table top, or on your lap. Use quilting thread; it is thicker than ordinary thread and is less likely to tangle. A small (#10 or #12) quilting needle will enable you to take small stitches. Cut the thread 20" long and tie a small knot. Starting about 1" from where you want the quilting to begin, insert the needle through the top and batting only. Gently tug on the knot until it pops through the quilt top and is caught in the batting. Take small, even, straight stitches through all layers.

To make small stitches, push the needle with a thimble on your middle finger. Insert the needle and push it straight down. Then rock the needle up and down through all layers "loading" three or four stitches on the needle. Pull the needle through, aiming toward yourself as you work. Place your other hand under the quilt and use your thumbnail to make sure the needle has penetrated all three layers with each stitch.

To end a line of quilting, make a single knot close to the quilt top and then take a 1" stitch through the top and batting only. Clip the thread at the surface of the quilt. When all the quilting is completed, remove the basting (except for the stitches around the edges). What a joyous moment this is!

BINDING

Trim the batting and backing even with the quilt top. Cut $1^3/4$" bias strips from the binding fabric. Seam the bias strips end to end to make strips that are long enough for each of the four edges of the quilt. Sew the strips about 4" longer than each edge of the quilt. Press a $1/4$" hem on one long edge of each strip. Center the unpressed edge of a strip on one edge of the quilt top, right sides together.

Sew through all layers, using a $1/4$" seam and being careful not to stretch the quilt or the binding. Begin and end at the seam line. Repeat on the remaining three edges of the quilt. Fold the binding to the back and blind-stitch the pressed $1/4$" hem in place. At the corners, trim and tuck in the end and stitch.

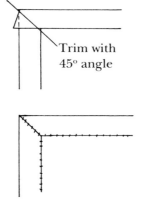

Trim with 45° angle

LABELING

Labeling your quilt is a nice finishing touch. You can embroider your name, city, and the date on the back of your quilt. If you have too much information to embroider, you can letter a label with a permanent pen on muslin or even type the information on muslin and stitch it to the back.

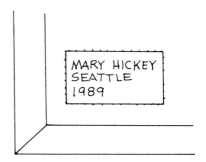

MARY HICKEY
SEATTLE
1989

Hasty Harvest by Mary Hickey, 1989, Seattle, Washington, 24" x 24". The unusual combination of fruit colors in turquoise, plum, mustard, and rose fit cheerfully into the tan basket. Careful cutting and placement of the thick and thin elements of the striped fabric create the woven look of the basket and the volume of the frame. The basket-weave fabric of the set triangles echoes the woven theme.

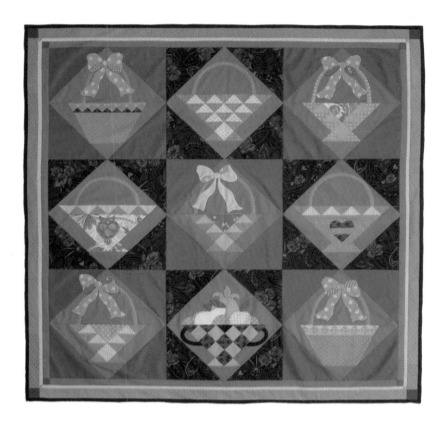

Madly Magenta by Laura Reinstatler, 1989, Seattle, Washington, 70" x 70".
Laura's expertise with color and her love of magenta is evident in this
celebration of baskets.

That Patchwork Place Publications

Angelsong by Joan Vibert
Baby Quilts from Grandma by Carolann Palmer
A Banner Year by Nancy J. Martin
Back to Square One by Nancy J. Martin
Christmas Memories—A Folk Art Celebration by
    Nancy J. Martin
Copy Art for Quilters by Nancy J. Martin
A Dozen Variables by Marsha McCloskey and
    Nancy J. Martin
Even More by Trudie Hughes
Feathered Star Quilts by Marsha McCloskey
Feathered Star Sampler by Marsha McCloskey
Happy Endings—Finishing the Edges of Your Quilt
    by Mimi Dietrich
Holiday Happenings by Christal Carter
Housing Projects by Nancy J. Martin
Little By Little: Quilts in Miniature
    by Mary Hickey
More Template-Free Quiltmaking by Trudie Hughes

My Mother's Quilts: Designs from the Thirties
    by Sara Nephew
Ocean Waves by Marsha McCloskey and Nancy J. Martin
One-of-a-Kind Quilts by Judy Hopkins
Pieces of the Past by Nancy J. Martin
Pineapple Passion by Nancy Smith and
    Lynda Milligan
Projects for Blocks and Borders by Marsha McCloskey
Reflections of Baltimore by Jeana Kimball
Small Quilts by Marsha McCloskey
Stars and Stepping Stones by Marsha McCloskey
Template-Free Quiltmaking by Trudie Hughes
Women and Their Quilts by Nancyann Johanson
    Twelker

For more information, send $2 for a color catalog
to That Patchwork Place, Inc., P.O. Box 118,
Bothell, WA 98041-0118. Many titles are available
at your local quilt shop.